APPLE PLUMPKIN
250+ AUTUMN ACTIVITIES

by dayle m. timmons

Fearon Teacher Aids

Lovingly dedicated to Wesley, the "apple" of my eye, and to my precious little "pumpkin," Courtney, and to Jimmy, who provides the sunshine for us all.

With special gratitude to each of the following for their many creative suggestions included in this unit:

Kristen VanValkenburg
Linda Sloan
Tinker Slack
Kerry Rogers
Maree Dawkins
Mary Pat Byrnes

Gail Long
Felicia Larson
Mary Catherine Dake
Jennifer Baldwin
Kathy Grimm
Lauren Werch

To Maree Dawkins and Ann Winfree for searching high and low for the books that are included in this unit. And especially to Donna Kellam, Sandy Price, Suzanne Oaks, and Laura Crooks, who have "nurtured the vine so that it might grow."

Editor: Susan Eddy

Fearon Teacher Aids
An Imprint of Modern Curriculum
A Division of Simon & Schuster
299 Jefferson Road, P.O. Box 480
Parsippany, NJ 07054–0480

2 3 4 5 6 7 8 9   TCS   01 00 99 98 97 96

CONTENTS

APPLES

PUMPKINS

INTRODUCTION

Leaves falling in vibrant fall colors, apples and pumpkins—for me, nothing in the world brings back so many fond, warm memories. I can still smell the hot apple cider simmering and that fresh pumpkin pie just out of the oven. It's one of my favorite times of the year.

Apples and Pumpkins is loaded with ideas and activities to use during this special season. The book includes two whole-language units with strong bases in literature and many phonics games and activities that can be easily integrated into science and social studies units. You may wish to study the growth of an apple tree through the seasons and label the parts of the apple and tree for a science unit. Or follow the adventures of Johnny Appleseed as part of a social studies unit. You can plant pumpkin seeds, watch the vines stretch and grow practically before your eyes, and see bees pollinate the yellow flowers. Before long, tiny green pumpkins have appeared. Cut open a mature pumpkin with children and there are more seeds to plant—the life cycle repeats.

The *Apples and Pumpkins* units are designed to stand alone. You may wish to begin the year with *Apples* and use *Pumpkins* as a Halloween alternative. Or simply enrich your traditional fall offerings with ideas from the book. There are more activities than you could possibly use in one season, so choose those that seem appropriate for your current crop of children. Next year, try some others. The activities span all learning styles and curriculum areas and are sure to provide hours of delightful, hands-on experiences. Enjoy!

d.m.t.

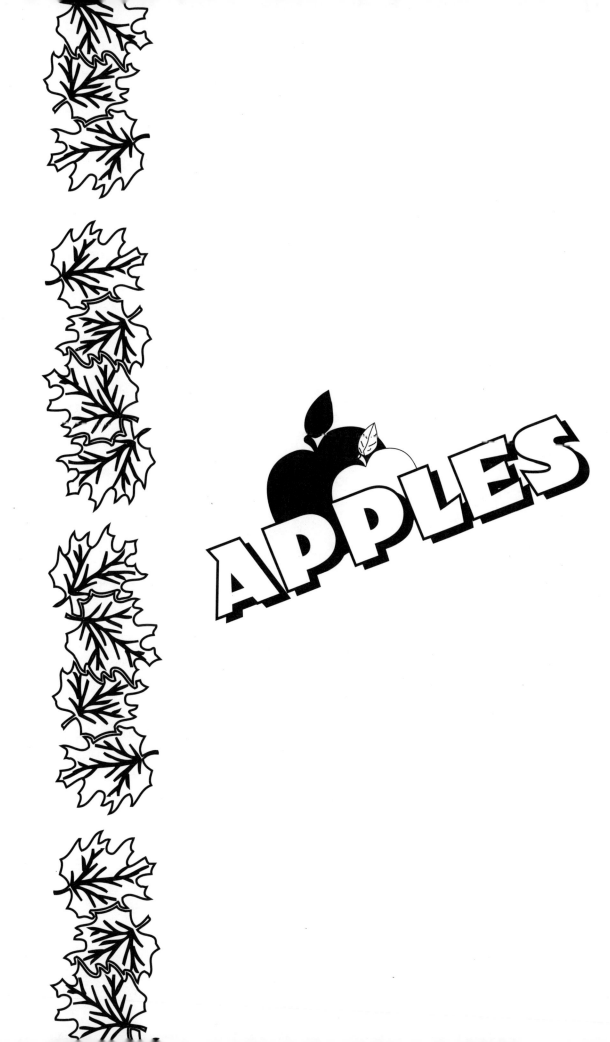

GETTING STARTED

Before you begin, write to:

International Apple Institute
6707 Old Dominion Drive, Suite 320
McLean, Virginia 22101
Telephone (703) 442–8850
Fax (703) 790–0845

The Apple Institute will furnish filmstrips, a VHS video, apple decals, curriculums, coloring books, and so on at nominal cost. They have many fine resources to add to this unit.

Meet with children in your class to find out what they already know about apples and what they would like to learn. Make a list of all the things that children say they know, correct or incorrect, about apples. For example:

Some apples are red and some are green.
Apples are fruit.

Then make a list of some things that they would like to find out. For example:

Where are most apples grown?
Why are apples good for you?

Put yourself in the learner role and add some of your own questions to the list. Decide on major concepts and understandings to develop based on the list you and your children create. Use the activities that follow to integrate concepts and goals into your unit.

Keep a chart of interesting facts about apples. Add a new fact each day. Three good resource books are *The Amazing Apple Book* by Paulette Bourgeois (Addison Wesley Publishing Company, 1987); *The Life and Times of the Apple* by Charles Micucci (Orchard Books, 1992); and *Apples: All About Them* by Alvin and Virginia B. Silverstein (Prentice Hall, 1976).

Here are some facts to get you started.

- There are more than 7,000 different types of apples.
- The first apple orchard in North America was planted in Boston, Massachusetts, in 1625.
- Our first president, George Washington, had a large apple orchard.
- The most famous apple sower was John Chapman, also known as Johnny Appleseed.
- The main apple-growing states in order are Washington, New York, Michigan, Pennsylvania, California, Virginia, and North Carolina.
- At least 40 states grow apples.
- Apples help quench your thirst because they are 85–95 percent water.
- Apples contain vitamins A and C, potassium, and pectin, which lowers cholesterol. They contain almost no fat. That is why we say, "An apple a day keeps the doctor away" and the newer version, "Two apples a day get the doctor's okay."
- The apple skin is what makes the apple smell so sweet.
- The Red Delicious apple is the most popular variety in the United States.
- Most apple trees do not bear fruit for the first 4–10 years.
- Most apple trees produce fruit for 40–50 years. Some will produce for 100 years!
- There are an estimated 3,000,000 apple trees in the United States.
- October is officially known as Apple Month because that is when the largest number of apples are picked.
- Most apples are still picked by hand.
- Mechanical pickers are used to shake apple trees. The apples that fall to the ground are used for juice and applesauce.
- More than half the apples grown are eaten fresh.
- The apple blossom is the state flower of Arkansas and Michigan.
- Crab apples are any apples less than two inches (five cm) in diameter.
- When one apple in a barrel spoils, the others will also rot quickly. That's where we get the saying, "One rotten apple spoils the barrel."
- Some apple trees are pruned in a Christmas-tree shape, so the upper limbs do not shade the lower limbs.

LITERATURE CONNECTIONS

Take a bite out of a good book! Add a bushel basket to your book center and fill it with books about apples. Ask children in your class and their parents to share books they might have at home, check the library, and go through your classroom library for a collection of "apple" books.

Share one or both of the following books with your children. Each book centers on the theme of things apple trees provide for us.

The Giving Tree by Shel Silverstein (Harper and Row, 1964).
A young boy visits an apple tree throughout his life. When the child is young, the tree provides apples to eat and branches to play on. As he gets older, it provides him with apples to sell and wood for a family home. When the boy reaches old age, the tree can offer only a stump to sit on. A tender story about loving and giving with simple line drawings.

Apple Tree Christmas by Trinka Hakes Noble (Dial Press, 1984).
In 1881, when their apple tree is felled by a storm just before Christmas, a young farm girl and her family discover that the tree was important to each of them for a different reason. A sweet family story with beautiful illustrations.

After reading either of these books, brainstorm with children things that come from trees and things that trees provide for us, such as shade, swings, a place to climb and sit, wood to burn for warmth, paper, pencils, houses, furniture, magazines, newspapers, fruit. Have each child choose one thing from the list to illustrate. Display the paintings or illustrations on a bulletin board entitled "The Giving Trees."

Here are some other fiction books that include apples in their theme.

Apple Picking Time by Michele B. Slawson (Crown Publishing, 1994).
A touching look at a young girl and her family who spend a fall day picking apples with others from their small town. Filled with beautiful pictures.

Applemouse by Ulrich Thomas (Hill and Wang, 1972).
The story of a little farm mouse who uses an apple as a home until he eats so much that it collapses. Illustrated with photographs.

The Mouse and the Apple by Stephen Butler (Tambourine Books, 1994).
Mouse is happily waiting for a ripe, red apple to drop from a tree. Hen, Goose, Cow, and Goat are waiting for the same apple. They all think up ways to make it drop but none of their ideas work so they give up and leave. Finally, the apple falls and mouse's patience is rewarded.

The Giant Apple by Ursel Scheffler (Carolrhoda Books, 1990).
The townspeople of Appleville decide to beat their neighbors from Beet Valley by growing the largest apple ever. They sacrifice all their other crops to grow a prize-winning apple but as winter comes, the townspeople begin to realize their foolishness.

How to Make an Apple Pie and See the World by Marjorie Priceman (Knopf, 1994).
This deliciously silly adventure begins with a trip to the market to buy ingredients for an apple pie. When the market is closed, a trip around the world gathers each ingredient from its native land. The finale is a grand apple pie.

Oats and Wild Apples by Frank Asch (Holiday House, 1988).
A calf and fawn meet and learn about each other's lives—the fawn eating wild apples in the forest and the calf eating oats in the barn. In the end, each prefers to return home and be near mother.

Ten Apples Up on Top by Theodore LeSieg (Dr. Seuss Beginner Books, Random House, 1961) available on filmstrip and cassette and in a cassette read-along version.
Three wacky characters parade around with different numbers of apples on their heads. A load of apples is overturned with some funny results.

Invite each child to draw an animal with a number of apples on top of the animal's head. Under each picture, children may fill in the phrase, "(Number) apples up on top of a (animal)!" Children may simply draw the apples or use a red bingo dabber or apple rubber stamp to represent the appropriate number of apples. Make a book cover and bind the drawings in numerical order for a class big book.

Although neither of the following books is about apples directly, they are absurdly silly and lots of fun.

2 apples up on top of a rabbit

Once Upon a Golden Apple by J. Little and M. Devries (Puffin Books, 1992).
A silly fractured fairy tale told under an apple tree.
Delightfully hilarious.

Rain Makes Applesauce by Julian Scheer (Holiday House, 1964).
A Caldecott Honor Book of silly talk.
It is a book of delicious absurdities, captivating scenes, and lyrical phrases that stretch the imagination. This is a fun book to "change up." Encourage children to think up absurdly silly sentences such as:

> The teacher stands on her head all day
> and rain makes applesauce.

> My hairbrush has wings and flies in the sky
> and rain makes applesauce.

Throw in, "Oh, you're just talking silly talk," every now and then. Invite children to illustrate their own absurd verses. Display on a bulletin board or bind together into a class big book.

Encourage children to read one or several best-loved apple stories.

The Golden Apples (from Greek mythology in which the apple tree bore golden apples of immortality).

The Story of William Tell (a legendary Swiss patriot who shot an apple off his son's head with a crossbow to defy a tyrant).

Snow White (the evil stepmother used a poisoned apple to put Snow White to sleep).

The Story of Sir Isaac Newton (who discovered the law of gravity while sitting beneath an apple tree).

There are books for each of these stories but some are too advanced for young readers. Simpler versions may be used as read-aloud books or, better yet, learn the stories and "tell" them to the class.

Johnny Appleseed, born in Leominster, Massachusetts, on September 26, 1774, was really named John Chapman. He lived during pioneer days and was said to be a tall, skinny fellow who walked barefoot, wore a pot on his head, and carried apple seeds in a pack on his back and a walking stick carved from an apple tree. He carried apple seeds and seedlings with him everywhere he went for more than 40 years, starting many small orchards in the Ohio Valley area. Some Native Americans considered him a medicine man. According to legend, he valued life and was never known to injure or kill any living thing except one rattlesnake, which he always regretted. John Chapman believed that one man could make a difference and he did. Johnny Appleseed was so beloved that many stories and legends about him have survived and spread. Some are probably true and others fabricated or simply exaggerated. Share some of the following books about Johnny Appleseed's life with your class. Many are good for reference and others for reading aloud (indicated with an*).

Better Known as Johnny Appleseed by Mabel Leigh Hunt (Lippincott, 1950).

Folks Call Me Appleseed John by Andrew Glass (Doubleday Books for Young Readers, 1995).

***John Chapman: The Man Who Was Johnny Appleseed* by Carol Greene (Childrens Press, 1991).

***Johnny Appleseed* retold and illustrated by Steven Kellogg (Morrow Junior Books, 1988).

Johnny Appleseed by Reeve Lindbergh (Little, Brown and Company, 1990).

Johnny Appleseed by Gertrude Norman (Putnam, 1960).

Johnny Appleseed by Louis Sabin (Troll, 1985).

Johnny Appleseed by Jan Gleiter and Kathleen Thompson (Raintree Children's Books, 1987).

Johnny Appleseed by Carol Beach York (Troll, 1980).

Johnny Appleseed and the Planting of the West by Gina Ingoglia (Disney Press, 1992).

Little Brother of the Wilderness: The Story of Johnny Appleseed by Meridel LaSueur (Knopf, 1947).

Restless Johnny: The Story of Johnny Appleseed by Ruth Holberg (Crowell, 1950).

**The Story of Johnny Appleseed* by Aliki (Simon and Schuster, 1963).

**The Story of Johnny Appleseed* by LaVere Anderson (Garrard Publishing, 1974).

The Value of Love: The Story of Johnny Appleseed by Ann Donegan Johnson (Value Communications, 1979).

"Johnny Appleseed: A Pioneer and a Legend." Booklet available from the International Apple Institute (see page 6).

After reading some books, have children help you make a simple time line of Johnny Appleseed's life. Start with his birth, death, and the time that he traveled planting apple trees. You can add other dates as you read about them. The following example of a time line is based on information from Andrew Glass's *Folks Call Me Appleseed John.*

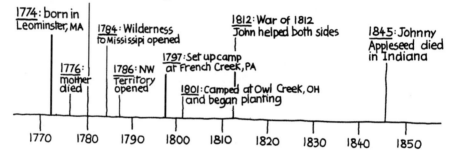

1780: father home from war, moved to Longmeadow, MA

1774: born in Leominster, MA

1784: Wilderness to Mississipi opened

1812: War of 1812 John helped both sides

1845: Johnny Appleseed died in Indiana

1776: mother died

1786: NW Territory opened

1797: Set up camp at French Creek, PA

1801: Camped at Owl Creek, OH and began planting

1770   1780   1790   1800   1810   1820   1830   1840   1850

Obtain a simple map of the eastern United States. Make line maps for each child or a larger map for the class. Help children identify Massachusetts, the state where Johnny Appleseed was born. Help them find and color states he planted apple trees in as you read about them (Steven Kellogg's *Johnny Appleseed* is a good resource for this activity).

After reading some books about Johnny Appleseed's life, help children make an apple-shaped class book about Johnny Appleseed. Cut apple-shaped front and back covers from red construction paper or tagboard. Cut white drawing-paper pages in the same shape. For each page, ask children to supply a fact about Johnny Appleseed's life, such as Johnny Appleseed wore a pot on his head, or Johnny Appleseed never wore shoes. Invite volunteers to illustrate each of the sentences.

Johnny Appleseed

Johnny Appleseed wore a pot on his head.

Johnny Appleseed was born in a house with a big apple tree.

Culminate your study by watching the 30-minute VHS video *Johnny Appleseed* (Rabbit Ears Productions, Rowayton, CT, 1992) or *The Legend of Johnny Appleseed*, which can be borrowed from the International Apple Institute (see page 6) for a small charge. This VHS video is a 15-minute original Walt Disney color production with enchanting animation and sound track. "Johnny Appleseed: Friend of Apple Lovers" stickers can be ordered for a minimal charge from the Apple Institute as well. Another filmstrip/cassette possibility is *Johnny Appleseed* (Society for Visual Education, Inc., Chicago, IL, 1993), which is 40 frames and runs about nine minutes. After you have shared a number of books about apples, invite children to write a story, dictate a story, and/or draw a picture story about apples. Here are some title suggestions.

The Great Apple Adventure
An Apple Was My Home
A Day With Johnny
　　Appleseed
The Magic Apple
The Biggest Apple Ever
The Great Apple
The Secret of the Hole in the
　　Apple
The Talking Apple

Worm's Little Red House
The Story of the Star Inside
The Applesauce Mystery
Red Is My Favorite Color
Seasons of the Apple Tree
The Apple Family
Bobbing for Apples
Climbing the Apple Tree
My Life as an Apple

🍎 Make a wall of apple words using a large tree shape cut from bulletin board paper. Precut red and green apple shapes (by hand, using a pattern, with an apple die-cut, or use Carson Dellosa's Big Tree Bulletin Board #CD-1701 with Apples #CD-5505). As words come up in reading and writing, add them to the apple tree. For example, tart, red, green, juicy, bite, orchard, seed, crunchy, sweet, fruit, harvest, cobbler, juice, cider, delicious, pie, healthy, tree, yummy. Add a few smiling green worms, just for fun! Encourage children to use the words as they write in their journals or other writing that they might be doing.

🍎 Play Apple Tree bingo using the words from your apple tree. Each child writes five words of his or her choice from the word wall on a sheet of paper or an apple shape. Call out words from the wall in random order. Children strike through the words on their lists as you call them. The first child to strike through all five words yells "Apple-O!" Continue with a new set of words for a new game.

🍎 Whenever you have a few spare minutes, call out a word from the wall and have a volunteer point to it. If correct, that child gets to call a word from the wall and select another student to find it. A good time filler! More mature children can divide the words into nouns, verbs, and adjectives or put them in alphabetical order.

🍎 Make a large apple-shaped journal for each child. Cut red or green construction-paper apple shapes on the fold for the front and back covers or use large apple-shaped notepad sheets. Cut plain white writing paper in the same shape for the children's pictures, words, and sentences. Encourage invented, temporary spelling.

RHYTHM 'N RHYME

 Sing these lyrics to the tune of "Here We Go 'Round the Mulberry Bush."

> Here we go 'round the apple tree,
> The apple tree, the apple tree.
> Here we go 'round the apple tree.
> _____ picks one for me.

Pick one child to stand in the middle of the circle. Invite the rest of the class to hold hands in a circle and walk one way around as they sing the first three lines. At the blank, the center child chooses a child from the circle. Children sing that child's name and he or she replaces the center child as they complete the song. The circle stops and reverses direction for a new verse.

Write this simple verse on sentence strips and read through it with the class. Have children watch you cut each strip into single words. Place the words in the correct order in a pocket chart and again read the verse together. Invite a volunteer to come up and turn one word backwards in its place while everyone else hides their eyes. Children open their eyes and try to guess the "mystery" word. Whoever guesses the word first gets the next turn.

 Teach this traditional favorite with motions.

> Way up high in the apple tree *(make two fists)*
> Two little apples smiling at me. *(turn fists toward face and
>   look at fists)*

I shook that tree as hard as I could *(pretend to shake tree)*
Down came the apples *(both hands stretched up over head and bring down)*
M-m-m-m! They were GOOD! *(rub tummy)*
(To the tune "That's what Campbell's soup is. M-m-m-m good!")
That's what apples are—, m-m-m-m GOOD!

Change up this rhyme by encouraging children to change the number and the word *little* to a color in the second line. For example, "Way up high in the apple tree, three green apples smiling at me." Place sticky notes over appropriate words to form new sentences. Children will start with realistic colors such as red, green, and yellow but will soon progress to more nonsensical choices such as blue and black apples. Encourage this word play. When children have tried a variety of colors and numbers, have each child choose one number and one color to illustrate. Duplicate the phrase "Way up high in the apple tree, _____ _____ apples smiling at me" on white paper. Children may fill in numbers and color words and then illustrate their pictures. Display on a bulletin board or bind together for a class book.

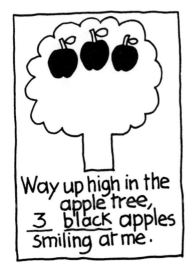

Way up high in the apple tree, 3 black apples smiling at me.

Teach this original rhyme by Linda Sloan.

Apple, apple way up high,
I can reach you if I try.
Climb a ladder,
Hold on tight.
Pick you quickly,
Take a bite.

Make a simple class book based on this rhyme. Write the words at the bottoms of three pages—two lines per page. Invite three volunteers to illustrate one page each. Have each child in the class draw a single apple for the cover. Cut around each of the apples and place on the cover collage style. Bind the book in traditional or accordion style for the class to enjoy.

LETTERS, LANGUAGE, AND PHONICS

Challenge children to name the following items. You can probably think of many more.

> Another red fruit.
> A red vegetable.
> A red drink.
> Something red and round like an apple.
> An animal that eats apples.
> Something bigger than an apple.
> Something smaller than an apple.
> Something about the same size as an apple.
> Something that would break if you threw an apple at it.
> Something heavier than an apple.
> Something lighter than an apple.
> Something softer than an apple.
> Something harder than an apple.
> Something you could balance on top of an apple.

 Help children practice saying the alphabet. Give each child an apple with a stem and invite them to find out their secret admirer by playing this game. As a child twists the stem, children sing the alphabet song. When the stem twists off, the child stops. The last letter sung is the first initial of the child's secret admirer. More mature children can twist the stem while saying the vowels a-e-i-o-u. When the stem twists off, they name someone with that vowel in his or her first name.

 Cut apple shapes from red tagboard or use apple-shaped notepad pages mounted on tagboard. Cut them in half and laminate to make apple puzzles. To make the game harder, make all the cuts the same. For an easier game, cut each apple in half, so it will only fit its match. On one apple half, write an uppercase letter. On the corresponding half, write the lowercase letter. By matching the letters, children put each apple puzzle together. Children can match some letters of the alphabet with pictures denoting initial or final consonant sounds.

Cut 26 apple shapes from red or green tagboard or use an apple-shaped notepad. Print one uppercase letter of the alphabet on each apple to use with large or small groups. Flash the letters in order and then in random order, having the class or individuals identify each letter.

When children are proficient at letter identification, challenge children to say the letters that come before or after the ones you flash. Leave the flash cards out so children can practice putting them in order. After children have mastered uppercase letters, add a set of lowercase letters for flashing, matching with uppercase, and ordering. More mature children can name words with the initial consonant sounds of the letters you flash.

Learn the nursery rhyme "A Apple Pie" by reading Tracey Campbell Pearson's version to the class (Dial Books for Young Readers, 1986). This fold-out book is a traditional ABC book that dates back to at least 1671, when it was quoted in the writings of a theologian. Since then, many versions have been published with Mother Goose rhymes. Pearson's updated version lists verbs in alphabetical order—all things you can do with an apple pie, such as "B bit it." Once children are familiar with the rhyme, hold up the alphabet flash cards in order and invite children to say the lines. Accept anything for each letter that makes sense.

A is for *apple*, so make an apple-shaped Apple Alphabet Book. Cut a cover from red construction paper (cut an apple shape on the fold) and add 26 apple-shaped white pages. Write a letter of the alphabet on each page and invite children to brainstorm apple-related words for each letter. They may then choose a page of the apple alphabet book to illustrate. More mature children might enjoy cutting pictures from magazines or drawing pictures of words that have the short *a* sound they hear in *apple*.

Write the upper or lowercase letters of the alphabet on long sentence strips with red crayon. Encourage children to trace each letter with their index fingers as they say the letters aloud—they will be able to feel the crayon texture. Then give children a small brush and red tempera paint or watercolor with which to paint over each letter. More mature children can paint the alphabet without the model (or they can paint their sight or spelling words).

Make an apple alphabet game played like bingo. Cut red and green apple shapes from tagboard. Write 4–8 letters of the alphabet on each shape. You might write all lowercase letters on one side of the tagboard and all uppercase on the other. Call the letters at random. Less mature children may need flash cards to match as you call the letters. Use red and green bingo chips, small apple-shaped erasers, or apple-flavored cereal bits for markers. For more mature children, write sight word vocabulary, color words, number words, or spelling words instead of the alphabet letters.

Have children brainstorm a list of words that start with *A*. With more mature children, discuss long and short *a* and put the words in two columns (you may need an "other" sound column for words that start with a different *A* sound, such as *above*). When possible, draw simple pictures next to words to help children remember them. Children may use white glue to write a large capital *A* on a 12" x 18" (30 cm x 45 cm) sheet of construction paper. Provide apple-flavored cereal bits for children to place on the glue to make an Apple A. Repeat with the lowercase *a*. Then have children copy words from your group list around their letters. (Children should only copy words they can read.)

🍎 Brainstorm a list of words for each of the letters *A-P-P-L-E*. Draw simple pictures by words when possible to help children remember. Then help children write an acrostic poem. Children can do this individually, in small cooperative groups, or as a teacher-directed group activity.

Apples
Perfect in a pie
Piece by piece
Little ice cream
on top
Everyone enjoys!

🍎 Cut several apple shapes from red tagboard and leaf shapes from green tagboard. Glue a piece of Velcro to each leaf and a matching piece to each apple where the leaf is to be attached. Children may match uppercase alphabet letters to lowercase, or match alphabet letters to pictures indicating initial or final consonant sounds or rhyming words.

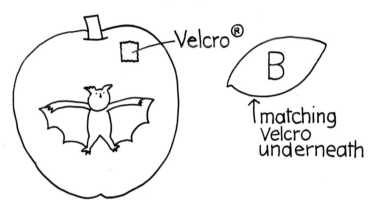

Velcro®

B

↑matching
Velcro
underneath

🍎 Help children practice classifying. Place category names on several baskets, such as clothing, furniture, things to read, things to write with, things that go (transportation), fruits, and people. Or use only food categories (fruits, vegetables, meats, drinks). Write items on individual apple shapes. Children sort the appropriate "apples" into each basket.

For more classifying practice, cut large tagboard apple shapes and label with category pictures, such as spoons, nuts, or things to write with. Collect real objects for each category. For example, for spoons, you might collect plastic spoons, teaspoons, measuring spoons, serving spoons, slotted spoons, and baby spoons. For nuts, you could use a plastic nut from an artificial arrangement, a real walnut, a pecan, a peanut, some shelled almonds, and a Brazil nut. Put the real items in a bushel basket and invite children to select items for each category and place them on the tagboard apples.

MATH AND SCIENCE

- Make a class apple number book. Cut an apple-shaped cover from red construction paper. Cut white pages in the same shape and write a number on each page. Use an apple stamp, cork, fingerprint with red washable ink, or a red bingo dabber to place the appropriate number of prints beside each number.

- Make apple trees for your flannel board. Use green felt for the tree tops and tan felt for the trunks. Write a number from 1 to 10 or higher on each trunk. Cut out red felt circles to represent apples. Children will place the appropriate number of apples on each tree. The same trees can be used for more mature children by using both green and red apples. Have children represent the number on the tree trunk with a combination of red and green apples and write an addition equation based on their representation.

$$3 + 1 = 4$$

- Have children tear strips of brown construction paper for tree trunks and larger pieces of green construction paper for tree tops. Invite them to write or trace numbers on their tree trunks. Then, using pregummed red dots or a cork dipped in red tempera, children may place the appropriate number of "apples" on their trees. Hang the trees in numerical order on a bulletin board entitled "Apple-licious." Teach children the following verse.

> **I see the apples all in a row.**
> **This is a number that I know.**

Each child may come to the front, point to his or her apple tree, and say the number on the tree trunk after the verse. The class then counts up to the number named and the verse is repeated until each child has had a turn.

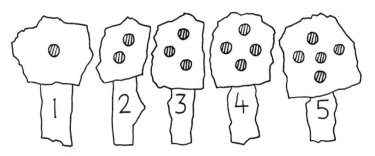

Collect tongue depressors and small apple stickers. Write a number from 1 to 10 or higher on each tongue depressor. Place the appropriate number of apple stickers on each tongue depressor and invite children to order the sticks numerically. For a variation, put the stickers on without numerals and have children match sticks to a numbered chart.

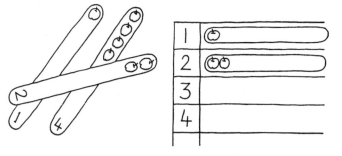

Help children practice writing and recognizing numerals. Write the numbers 1 to 10 or higher in an accordion book for each child. Have children use red bingo dabbers (available with bingo supplies) to dab along the lines, washable red stamp pads and their fingers, or an apple rubber stamp or cork.

Draw pictures of apple trees and bushel baskets on tagboard. Write a number on each tree or basket and have children use large red pompoms to count the appropriate number of "apples" onto each tree or basket. More mature children may use red and green pompoms and write addition problems based on the number of red and green apples they placed on each tree.

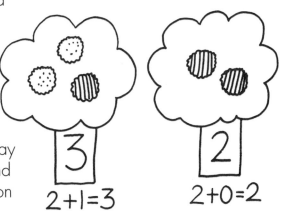

 Practice counting with these words to the tune of "Ten Little Angels in the Band."

> There was 1, there were 2, there were 3 little apples,
> There were 4, there were 5, there were 6 little apples,
> There were 7, there were 8, there were 9 little apples,
> 10 little apples on the tree.
>
> Oh wasn't that a day at the or-chard, at the or-chard,
>   at the or-chard.
> Wasn't that a day at the or-chard.
> 10 little apples on the tree.

Pop up one finger for each number. Keep a steady beat by clapping on the last three lines.

Cut 10 apple shapes from felt for your flannelboard and put up an apple for each number as you sing the rhyme. Or use numerals on the flannelboard and sing the song putting up the correct numerals.

Using washable markers, write the numbers 1 to 10 on each child's fingernails—one number on each nail. Be sure the numbers are "right side up" and read from left to right. Have children hold up the appropriate numbers as you sing.

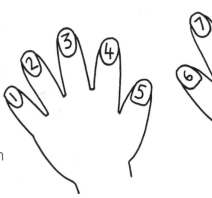

Make ten apple-shaped cutouts with head holes from green and red tagboard. Children may stand up with their apples as you sing their numbers in the song.

Make a class book to illustrate the song. Cut apple shapes, use construction paper die-cut apples, or have children draw and color apples and then cut them out—enough to illustrate each verse of the song. Place the words for one number and the appropriate number of apples on each page. Add a cover and title page and bind together.

There was 1

There were 2

There were 3 little apples

Write the song on chart paper and provide apple-shaped sticky notes with number words—one number word per sticky note. Children may place sticky notes over the corresponding numerals as the song is sung.

Take snapshots of children holding apples (each holding one apple) or peering through apple-shaped cutouts (see above). First, take a picture of one child, then two children, then three children, and so on up to 10. Laminate and leave out. Individuals and small groups will enjoy ordering the pictures from 1 to 10. Make large +, −, and = signs for children to use with the pictures to make simple addition and subtraction problems.

Make some large dot-to-dot apples with numbers appropriate for your class and laminate. Encourage children to connect the dots with red or green water-based markers and then clean the laminate for the next child. Children may also enjoy making dot-to-dot apples for each other.

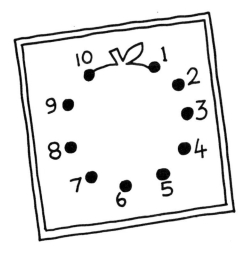

Make "Number Apples" for snack time. You will need:

1 apple per 2–3 children

peanut butter

raisins

Core the apples, cut cored apples into slices (to look like doughnuts), and place on small paper plates. Put peanut butter in the center holes and have children count out a predetermined number of raisins to stick on top of the peanut butter. Practice subtraction by saying to the class, "Eat one raisin. How many do you have left? This time, eat two . . ." and so on. Now that's apple-tizing!

Teach your class this original fingerplay by Kristen VanValkenburg about "Five Little Apples," which helps young children conceptualize subtraction.

> 5 little apples in a backpack by my door,
> I ate 1 and then there were 4.
> 4 little apples that I now see,
> Daddy took 1 and then there were 3.
> 3 little apples on their way to school,
> The teacher ate 1 and then there were 2.
> 2 little apples on the ledge in the sun,
> In crawled a worm and then there was 1.
> 1 little apple waiting by and by,
> My teacher cut it up and baked it in a pie!

Cut five apples for your flannel board or illustrate the rhyme with apple ornaments or real apples. Put out the five apples and remove one for each verse. Use verbal cloze by stopping after ". . . and then there were _____" and have children fill in the numbers.

Make an apple mitt to illustrate the rhyme. Use a commercial mitt or make your own from a garden glove with Velcro fastened to each finger. Make five apples from large red pompoms. Hot glue small pieces of brown pipe cleaner for stems and green felt leaves to each apple. Self-stick the matching Velcro to the backs of the pompoms. Place all five "apples" on the mitt and remove one at a time to illustrate the rhyme.

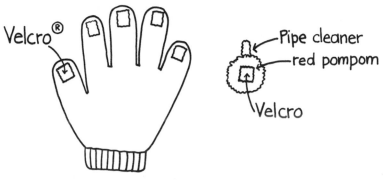

Challenge more mature children to write subtraction problems for the rhyme, such as $5 - 1 = 4$ for the first sentence.

Make single strips for each word and punctuation mark in the rhyme and distribute to children. Display one sentence of the rhyme at a time and invite children to come up and create the sentence. Help them stand in the correct order, holding their words or punctuation marks in front of their bodies. Children in their seats may read the completed sentence. Continue with the next sentence.

Have children sort the words you have cut out by length (number of letters in each word). Make a vertical line of consecutive numbers on the chalkboard. Children may count the letters in their words and place their cards beside the appropriate numbers. Discuss the graph they have created.

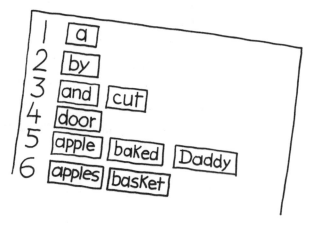

Another way to sort the words you have cut up is by initial or final letters. Write letters of the alphabet across the bottom of a chalkboard and have children place their words above the appropriate beginning or ending letter. Discuss the graph. How many *A* words? *B* words? Which letter of the alphabet has the most words? No words?

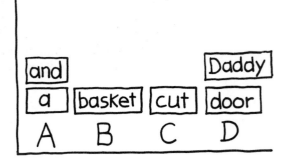

Make an apple counting game by cutting apple shapes from tagboard. Write a number from 1 to 10 or higher on each apple. Use apple seeds as counters (or dried black beans, sometimes called turtle beans) and have children place the appropriate number of apple seeds on each apple.

Practice position words with children. Cut out an apple and a worm for each child and laminate or have children make their own apples and worms to bring to the circle. Call out phrases such as, "Place the worm on the apple," "Place the apple beside the worm," "Place the worm under the apple," "Place the worm in front of the apple," and so on. Or try these: "Put the apple under your chin," "Put the worm between your ears," "Put the apple between your knees," "Put the worm on top of your feet," "Eat the worm!" (Just kidding!)

Practice estimating with children. Draw a large apple shape on a piece of tagboard. Cut an apple in half and invite children to guess how many prints will fit around the perimeter of the apple. Write each estimate on an apple-shaped piece of paper or sticky note. As children watch, dip the apple in red paint and make prints around the perimeter of the apple shape. Compare the estimates with the real number. Now have children guess how many prints it will take to fill the inside of the apple. Follow the same procedure. Be sure to compare the real number with the estimates.

Invite children to weigh apples on a balance scale. Provide two or three varieties of small apples. Place a sticker on each apple for identification purposes. Put out some counting bears as well. Children may count how many bears it takes to balance each apple. Which apple weighs more? Which apple weighs less? Do any of the apples weigh the same?

Provide a food or postage scale and a little over a pound of apples. Children may weigh individual apples, first predicting how much each one will weigh. For more mature children, cut the apple they have weighed in half and challenge them to estimate how much one-half will weigh. Which will weigh more—the half apple or whole apple? Review the fact that 16 ounces = 1 pound. Encourage children to use the scale to decide how many apples make a pound. Is it always the same number?

Show the class pictures of apple trees. Invite children to draw apple trees and label the parts: roots, trunk, branch, twig, flower, leaf, fruit.

Read Gail Gibbon's *The Seasons of Arnold's Apple Tree* (Harcourt Brace Jovanovich, 1984) to your children. This delightful book describes and illustrates an apple tree in all four seasons of the year. Invite children to draw apple trees in all four seasons. Fold sky blue construction paper in fourths so children may illustrate one season in each section. You may wish to provide a model, discussing each of the seasons as you draw.

 Share several of the following books with children. Then divide them into four groups—one for each season. Each child in each group may draw an apple tree illustration for the given season. Encourage children to add animals and seasonal activities to their drawings. Place the illustrations on a bulletin board divided into four sections: spring, summer, fall, and winter.

Apple Tree by Peter Parnall (Macmillan, 1988).
> The story of an old gnarled apple tree and how it grows and provides for a variety of animals throughout the seasons.

Look at an Apple by Cliff and Bernice Moon (The Wright Group, 1992).
> For the youngest reader (K–1) with a single picture and illustration for each season. Simple words and pictures about the life of an apple.

An Apple a Day by Melvin Berger (Newbridge Communications, 1993).
> A Macmillan's Early Science big book with simple text and beautiful photographs of all main science ideas in this unit.

How Do Apples Grow? by Betsy Maestro (HarperCollins, 1992).
A "Let's Read and Find Out Science Book." Simple prose and colorful pictures. Describes the apple tree throughout the seasons, parts of the apple blossom and apple, the process of fertilization and pollination, and different varieties of apples.

The Apple Tree by Lynley Dodd (G. Stevens, 1985).
Two children spend the year anticipating the fruit their apple tree will bear, only to have a wily thief upset their plans. Shows an apple limb throughout the seasons. Simple pictures and text.

Apple Tree! Apple Tree! by Mary Blocksma (Childrens Press, 1983).
Simple rhyming text follows the apple tree through the seasons. Part of the "Just One More" series.

The Life and Times of the Apple by Charles Micucci (Orchard Books, 1992).
Clear, concise text accompanied by detailed and labeled illustrations. Includes many interesting facts as well as life cycle, growing practices, history, and apple lore.

From Seed to Applesauce by Hannah Lyons Johnson (Lothrop, Lee, and Shepard, 1977).
Book of photographs with simple words that shows the seasons of the apple tree. A recipe for applesauce is included.

Apples by Rhonda Nottridge (Carolrhoda Books, 1991).
Good general resource. Describes different types of apples with excellent drawings, growing apples, enemies of the apple tree, the route from farm to store, and making cider. Three recipes included.

An Apple Tree Through the Year by Claudia Schnieper (Carolrhoda Books, 1987).
Great photographs of apple trees throughout the year. Share pictures and have children identify the season and what is happening in each photograph.

Apple Trees by Sylvia A. Johnson (Lerner Publications, 1983).
Good reference. Details about trees in each season plus lots of color photos.

🍎 Teach children this nursery rhyme that illustrates a growing apple tree:

> Once I found an apple seed,
> And stuck it in the ground.
> When I came to look at it,
> A tiny sprout I found.
> The shoot grew up and up each day,
> It soon became a tree.
> I picked the rosy apples then
> And ate them with my tea.

🍎 Write the rhyme on chart paper and point to each word as you read it, using an apple pointer to reinforce left-to-right progression. You can make an apple pointer by hot gluing a small apple ornament to a dowel (push an end-cap eraser onto the other end) or glue a flat wooden or paper apple to the end of a ruler or yardstick. Leaving the pointer out will encourage children to use it to "read" the rhyme just as you have done.

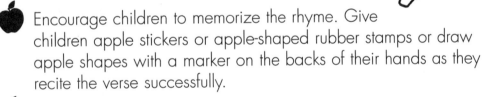

🍎 Encourage children to memorize the rhyme. Give children apple stickers or apple-shaped rubber stamps or draw apple shapes with a marker on the backs of their hands as they recite the verse successfully.

🍎 Have children role-play the poem by pretending to be small seeds (make balls on the floor), beginning to grow into tiny shoots (squatting), becoming full-grown trees (standing with arms spread), and then pretending to eat the apples.

🍎 Turn the verse into a class book. Have children illustrate the growing tree with a sequence of pictures for each two lines: the seed in the ground, the sprout, the tree with apples, and a child picking the apples or having them with tea. Pages may be individual or accordion style. Write the words from the rhyme for

each page or panel of the book. Volunteers may draw or paint the illustrations. Add a cover, title page, and a "getting to know the author(s)" page. Put the book in the book center.

Once I found an apple seed And stuck it in the ground.

When I came to look at it, A tiny sprout I found.

The shoot grew up and up each day, It soon became a tree.

I picked the rosy apples then and ate them with my tea.

If apples are grown in your area, bring in a branch of real apple blossoms. Otherwise, look for apple blossoms in pictures or artificial apple blossoms. The apple blossom has five petals that first appear pale pink but become white when fully developed. Some start out as deep pink or even purplish. The blossoms appear after the leaves and usually grow in clusters of five. After sharing pictures of apple blossoms, blossom clusters, and apple trees filled with blossoms, invite children to draw pictures of apple blossoms or blossoming trees.

Note: A tree grown from a seed from your favorite variety of apple might eventually produce fruit but the fruit might not be exactly like the apple that the seed came from. Apple trees bear fruit when they are cross-pollinated, which means the pollen from one apple blossom joins with the pollen of another. The resulting fruit has characteristics of both parent

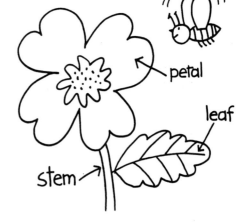

apples. Usually in a commercial orchard, many trees of one variety are grown together. You must have more than one apple tree to produce cross-pollination and apples. Bees are responsible for most apple pollination. Some growers even place beehives in their apple orchards.

Apples are harvested in late summer and early fall. Apples for eating are picked by hand and placed in a bag worn by the picker. A machine is used to shake apple trees that fall to the ground and are used for applesauce and juice. Apples are taken to cold storage, where they can be kept for a year. This allows us to have fresh apples all year long. Children will enjoy the following books about apple-picking time.

Apples and Pumpkins by Anne Rockwell (Scholastic, 1989). This simple book for the youngest readers tells about a family trip to Comstock Farm to pick apples and pumpkins. The day ends with the carving of a jack-o'-lantern for Halloween.

Picking Apples and Pumpkins by Amy and Richard Hutchings (Scholastic, 1994). Describes a family's day picking apples at the orchard and selecting pumpkins in the pumpkin patch. The children end their day by helping make apple pie. Beautifully photographed.

Apple Picking Time by Michele B. Slawson (Crown Publishers, 1994). A realistic look at a day of picking apples with beautiful illustrations and a touching family story.

 Bring in different types and colors of apples or have parents send them in. Tell children the story "The Little Red House" from *Easy-to-Tell Stories for Young Children* by Annette Harrison (National Storytelling Press, 1992) or the fantasy apple star story written 50 years ago by Georgia schoolteacher Madge Bigham (found in "Life Story of the Apple," *Apples: All About Them* by Alvin and Virginia B. Silverstein, Prentice Hall, 1976). Both these delightful stories talk about the "star" inside the apple. Or tell the original story below.

Once upon a time there lived a little boy named Wesley. Outside his window grew the most beautiful apple tree. It gave the most delicious apples in all the land. People came from all over to taste the wonderful apples and Wesley gave them freely to all who asked. One day, the rain stopped and there came a terrible drought in the land. Plants and trees began to die. Water had to be rationed so that each person was only given what was needed to survive. Wesley knew that his apple tree would not survive without water, so secretly he shared half his water with the tree. Slowly, all the apple trees in the land began to wither and

33

die—all except Wesley's tree. One glorious day, the rains returned. But it was too late for most of the apple trees. Only Wesley's tree had survived. People finally realized the great sacrifice that this courageous child had made to save his tree and provide apples for everyone. The heavens parted and a beautiful apple fairy in a white flowing gown sprinkled with sparkling apples came down and spoke, "Wesley, because you have sacrificed so much for so many, I will take a star from the heavens. From this day forth, all apples will have a star inside to remind us of all you have given." *(Cut an apple in half to display the star.)* And that is how apples got their stars.

🍎 Before cutting apples open, have children estimate how many seeds they might find inside the apple. Cut the apple through the middle to see the "star." The core of the apple is divided into five sections which usually contain two seeds each. Compare children's estimates with the seeds you count.

🍎 Have each child take half an apple with a star and use it to draw a likeness of how the inside of the apple looks using crayons, markers, or colored pencils.

🍎 Bring in several different varieties of apples. Encourage children to decide how deep they think the color goes in each apple. Cut a small wedge from each one and have children examine them with a magnifying glass. Ask children if some varieties have thicker skins than others. It's the skin that contains the delicious apple smell.

🍎 Bring in three different types of apples, including red, yellow, and green apples, or have parents send them in. Give each child a slice of each apple. On a sheet of chart paper, write the words children use to describe each apple, such as crunchy, soft, sweet, tart, hard. Ask children which

Favorite Apple

red	Aggie	Roy
green	Susan	
yellow		

apple they like best and graph the results with paper apple shapes. Discuss the results: "Which apple is the favorite?" "Did more children like red apples or green apples?" "How many children liked red/green apples?" "How many more children liked red apples than liked green apples?" And so on.

COOKING

Review apple cooking vocabulary with children: *core* (remove the middle while keeping the apple whole), *slice* (cut into thin pieces), and *peel* (remove the skin). If possible, bring in or ask parents to loan an apple corer, an apple corer-slicer, and/or an apple peeler-corer-slicer that attaches to the table and works with a hand crank.

Make applesauce with children. But before you start, ask them how they think applesauce is made. Write down the ingredients they think they will need and compare them to the list below, which you have prewritten on chart paper.

Applesauce

1/4 cup apple juice
2 cups cut-up apples (no skin)
honey to taste
cinnamon

You may wish to divide children into groups of two to four and have groups make their own applesauce. Children may peel and chop their own apples with a plastic or "pumpkin" knife. Be sure they get the seeds out. Pour the juice, apples, and honey into a blender or food processor. Have children blend to desired consistency. Sprinkle with cinnamon if desired. For cooked applesauce, you will need about one pound of apples for each cup of applesauce. Children cut their apples into chunks (peeled or unpeeled), remove seeds, and add a little honey (a little lemon juice is optional) and cook on low until soft. Sprinkle with cinnamon. Eat warm or cooled.

Children may decide how many cups or bowls and spoons you will need to serve the applesauce. Hannah Lyons Johnson's *From Seeds to Applesauce* (Lothrop, Lee, & Shepard, 1977) includes a recipe for applesauce and is a nice book to read after making the applesauce to explain the entire process. Read the Caldecott Honor Book *Rain Makes Applesauce* by Julian Scheer while you enjoy your applesauce.

Prepare apple pie for snack using prepared frozen pie or invite a parent to come in and make apple pie from scratch in your room. Children may come and go to help with the preparations as interests dictate. After enjoying the pie (with ice cream!), read *A Apple Pie*, illustrated by Tracey Campbell Pearson (Dial Books for Young Readers, 1986), a delightful traditional ABC rhyme, or the beautifully photographed *Picking Apples and Pumpkins* by Amy and Richard Hutchings (Scholastic, 1994), which describes picking apples and making them into a pie. Ask if parents have other favorite apple recipes that they would like to come and make in the class.

Read Gail Gibbon's *The Seasons of Arnold's Apple Tree*. After reading the book, have the class make "Arnold's Apple Pie." The recipe is included in the book.

Read the deliciously silly *How to Make Apple Pie and See the World* by Marjorie Priceman (Knopf, 1994), which begins with a trip to the market to buy the ingredients for an apple pie. When the market is closed, a trip around the world rounds up the ingredients. The finale is a grand apple pie from a simple recipe you may wish to try with the class.

Hot apple cider will make your room smell wonderful!

Hot Apple Cider

1/2 cup brown sugar or honey to taste
1/4 teaspoon salt
2 quarts apple cider or juice
1 teaspoon whole allspice
1 teaspoon whole cloves
3 inches stick cinnamon

juice of 1 lemon
juice of 4 oranges
dash nutmeg

Place the cloves and allspice in a tea ball. Pour all the other ingredients into a pot. Add the tea ball. Cover and simmer for 20 minutes, leave to slow cook in a Crock-Pot, or put through any automatic coffee-maker or percolator (putting the spices where you normally put the coffee). Serve warm with orange slices floating on top. Have some popcorn too! Makes a great snack after playing in the cold or snow.

Try the following snack with your hot apple cider.

Apple Snack

3 Tbs. butter or margarine, melted
1/2 tsp. apple pie spice
2 cups oyster crackers
4 cups popped popcorn
1 cup dry-roasted peanuts

Add apple pie spice to melted butter or margarine. Combine dry ingredients. Add butter mixture and toss until well coated. Makes 15–18 servings.

 Look for packaged apple muffin or bread mixes on the market and just follow the directions on the box. These quick muffins are super-easy and make a great snack.

 Make these easy and delicious apple cookies with your class.

Apple Cookies

Apple Newtons™ (like Fig Newtons™ but filled with apple)
white powdered sugar

Cut each Apple Newton into thirds. Pour some powdered sugar into a plastic zipper bag. Add a few Newton sections and have children shake, shake, shake. Take out of the bag and enjoy! Looks so nice, but so-o-o-o easy.

 Make dried apples, which is the way that people kept apples to eat year-round long ago.

Dried Apples

1 apple per child
string
optional: water and lemon juice

Children may peel and core their own apples (optional) and cut into slices 1/8 to 1/4-inch thick with plastic knives. Soaking apples in 2 cups water mixed with 1/4 cup lemon juice will keep them from turning too brown. If apples have been cored, children may string the slices through the center holes (or use needles and thread to go through the meat of the apples) and hang in the warmest, driest part of your room. Be sure none of the apples are touching—they should be about nine inches apart.

Apples should be ready to eat in about a week (if mashed, no juice comes out). Apple rings can also be microwaved to dry. Arrange rings on a paper towel, so they are not touching and cook on *defrost* for 35–45 minutes. Store extras in an airtight glass jar or paper bag. Be sure to dry some extra apples to hang on a tree outside for the birds to eat. You may also add green or red ribbons to individual slices for holiday ornaments. For additional enrichment:

🍎 Have children predict what they think will happen when the apple slices are left to dry. Write their predictions down and compare them to what actually occurs.

🍎 Dip some apple slices in lemon juice and keep others undipped. Watch the differences. What does the lemon juice do?

🍎 Compare the dried slices with fresh-cut slices. How are they the same and how are they different? Make two lists based on children's observations.

🍎 Bring in apple chips for snack and discuss how they are the same and how they are different from the dried apples you made. How is the taste different? The texture? The smell? Try the apple chips with caramel or peanut butter dip made especially for fruit.

🍎 Have children make apple sandwiches for snack one day.

Apple Sandwiches

2–4 apple slices per child
peanut butter

Have children core their apples and slice them with plastic knives into "donuts" about 1/4 to 1/2-inch thick. Help them use tongue depressors, craft sticks, or plastic knives to spread peanut butter on one slice and place another apple slice on the top.

🍎 For a yummy, easy snack, try slicing apples and dipping them in caramel, peanut butter, or chocolate dip made especially for dipping fruit.

🍎 Use prepared candied apple sets or caramel sheets to make super candied or caramel apple snacks on sticks.

🍎 If your children bring their own snacks to school, send home a note to their families asking them to send in apple snacks all week. Include suggestions such as applesauce, fresh green/red/yellow apples, apple pie, apple turnovers, apple juice, apple cake and muffins, apple chips, and apple bread. Keep a running list of all the different apple snacks children bring in. Children may wish to "show and tell" their apple snacks.

🍎 Play "Pass the Apple" right before snack time. You will need an apple (real or artificial) and children seated in a circle. Play some music and invite children to pass the apple. When the music stops, the child holding the apple gets his or her snack. Continue until all children have their snacks.

Explore apples with children. Encourage them to look closely at the inside and outside, to listen to the sounds of biting and chewing an apple, and to smell, feel, and taste an apple. Then have each child dictate a five senses poem about apples.

Apples smell _____.

Apples look _____.

Apples feel _____.

Apples sound_____.

Apples taste_____.

Write each child's dictation on an apple shape and display on a bulletin board entitled "Apples Make Sense!"

MANIPULATIVES

● Put out apple-shaped cookie cutters with your red or green play dough. Cut solid-color place mats in halves or quarters and write a number on each section. Or cut plain green or brown vinyl place mats into tree shapes and write a number on each tree. Encourage children to cut apples from play dough to match the numbers on the place mats using the apple cookie cutters. Or have children make apples by rolling balls of play dough.

● Put red or green food coloring in your water table or in a large dishpan of water. If you don't have a see-through table, provide clear, plastic containers for measuring and pouring. Cut some compressed sponge or colorful "fun foam" into apple shapes to float in the water table (these can also be die-cut). Add some tongs and invite children to pick up the apples with the tongs and put into bowls or sand pails.

● Ask children if they think apples will float in your water table or tub. Make a T-graph of *yes* and *no* responses. Children may record their answers with clip clothespins. Float some apples of different colors and sizes. Leave the apples in the water table for the rest of the day with some wooden spoons, ladles, and slotted spoons for children to use to scoop the apples.

Will the apple float?

Yes ☺   ☹ No

Juan

Rosie

● On the following day, ask children whether they think peeled apples will float. Peel the apples and place in the water table. Note any brown or bruised spots as you are peeling and discuss these with the children.

🍎 Place apples in the water table or tub and invite children to bob for apples. To make it easier, keep the water shallow, so children can actually trap the apples against the bottom. To make it harder, add more water. Be sure each child gets at least one apple.

🍎 Look for apples with stems. Hang apples from the ceiling or outside from an overhang or tree limb, so that an apple hangs in front of each child's mouth. Challenge children to eat the apples with their hands behind their backs. Have your camera ready! Both bobbing for apples and eating apples from strings are games that were brought to America by the English settlers.

🍎 Make red or green sand for your sand table by adding liquid or paste food coloring to a bottle of rubbing alcohol. Pour the entire contents into your sand and mix together (wear plastic gloves or use a garden trowel to avoid staining hands). The sand will dry by the end of the day. Sprinkle a little red or green glitter in the sand just for fun! Or look for apple-shaped confetti to sprinkle into the sand. When you are finished with the unit, have children use colanders or sand sifters to clean out the confetti.

🍎 Make apple-shaped lacing cards. Cut apple shapes from red and green tagboard (or use sheets from a large apple-shaped notepad glued to tagboard). Laminate and punch holes around the outside. Invite children to lace shoelaces around the perimeters of the apples. Sometimes you can find matching seasonal shoelaces.

🍎 Use the overhead projector as a center. Make a transparency of a simple drawing of two or three apples. Put the projector on the floor and add a supply of white paper and markers. Turn on the overhead, so the apple picture is projected on a wall (you may wish to cover the wall area with a large sheet of bulletin board paper, so stray marks will not get on the wall or project the picture on a chalkboard and have children use colored chalk). Children may hold or tape their papers to the wall and trace around the apples to make their own apple pictures.

ARTS AND CRAFTS

🍎 Make a list of several types of apples and discuss their characteristics. A list can be obtained from the International Apple Institute (see page 6). Here are the top ten sellers: Red Delicious, Golden Delicious, McIntosh, Rome Beauty, Granny Smith, Jonathan, York Imperial, Stayman, Newtown Pippin, Winesap. Other interesting names: Crispin, Gala, Gingergold, Idared, Jonagold, Lodi, Melrose, Northern Spy, Paulared, Spartan, Twenty-ounce, Wealthy, Tydeman Early. Encourage children to make up stories about why and how each apple might have gotten its name. Children may make up names for new types of apples, such as Timmons' Tart, give some characteristics (red, large, tart, good for eating), and draw pictures of how their apples would look.

🍎 Have children tear red or green construction paper into small pieces to glue onto small round paper plates to make apples. Show them how to add brown pieces for stems and green pieces for leaves. Take snapshots of each child and cut out just the heads or use photocopies of school pictures. Children may glue their photos to the centers of their apples. Make a large tree on a bulletin board and display the apples on the tree with the title, "The Apples of My Eye."

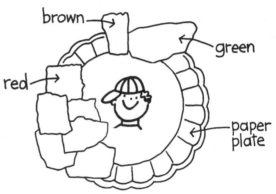

🍎 Have children make apple hats using die-cut apples in red, green, and yellow. Children may glue apples along sentence strips in any pattern they like. Green or red glitter may be sprinkled over the apple cutouts if you like. After the glue has dried, staple the ends of the sentence strips to fit each child's head.

Put out whole apples of different shapes and colors, apples cut in half the long way, and apples cut in half showing the "star." Talk with children about how the apples differ, the various shapes, colors, and so on. Invite children to choose several different versions to illustrate using crayons.

Pour red, yellow, and green tempera paint over a sponge on a Styrofoam tray. Cut several small apples in half (cut some the long way and some across, so the star shows), wipe off the excess juice, and let them sit for about an hour. Put one apple half in each color. Apples are hard to hold—corn-on-the-cob holders provide a better grip. Children may use the apples to dip into paint and print on construction paper in any pattern desired.

Use the small apples from the previous activity and tempera paint to make bulletin-board borders. Print apples on strips of construction paper or use wide adding machine tape. Print them randomly or decide on a pattern for children to follow, such as red/red/green.

Put red and green or yellow paint at the easel. Discuss with children that apples are round (the shape of a circle) and encourage children to paint just one large apple or several. Put out a few real apples for children to study as they paint.

More mature children may make apple-cinnamon jewelry. Mix 1/2 cup ground cinnamon (67 grams, 2.37 ounces) with 6 Tbs. applesauce for enough dough to make about 18 small ornaments or pins. Add more cinnamon if needed to make a nonsticky dough. Place dough on a smooth surface and roll out with a rolling pin or wooden cylinder block. Cut shapes with small cookie cutters such as hearts or bears. Poke holes in the tops with a toothpick. Place on a paper plate and microwave on high for two minutes. Turn and microwave another 30 seconds if needed until shapes are hard. Cool completely and air dry for a couple of days. Run thin pieces of ribbon through the holes for necklaces or ornaments, or hot glue pin fasteners to the backs to make pins. Your room will smell wonderful!

Show children how to make apple wreaths from construction paper. Use paper plates with centers cut out as bases for the wreaths. Have children cut red, green, or yellow apple shapes from construction paper using patterns or use construction paper apple die-cuts. Discuss patterns such as red/green/red/green or red/yellow/green or have children glue apples around the ring in any arrangement they choose. Add colorful ribbons. A paper clip taped or hot glued to the underside makes a nice hanger.

Make apple centerpieces. Cut two apple shapes from white construction paper for each child or have children cut their own. Show children how to sponge-paint the two apples using pieces of sponge attached to clothespins and red, green, or yellow paint. Children may use just one color on each apple or a combination of colors. Sprinkle glitter on the apple shapes while still wet. When both sides have dried, glue them back-to-back, adding stems cut from brown construction paper between the two shapes. Add craft sticks or tongue depressors to the bottoms of the apples. (Optional: Cover each apple on a stick with clear or tinted plastic wrap and tie with coordinating curling ribbons.) Put several apples in a flowerpot, which may be painted or sponged with apple shapes. To help the apples stay firmly in place, push an upside-down Styrofoam® bowl into the bottom of the flowerpot and insert the apple sticks through the Styrofoam. Add old Easter grass, Spanish moss, or straw to the pot. Makes a great centerpiece for Fall Open House or for an Apple Luncheon for parents.

FIELD STUDY

- Visit an apple orchard where children may pick apples. Purchase some apple butter or fresh apple cider if available. Be sure to take pictures of the apple trees and children picking apples.

- Place photographs of the trip in a picture album and invite children to write captions for each picture.

- Make a sentence-strip class book about the field experience. Ask each child to finish the sentence, "At the apple orchard, (child's name) liked _____ ." Encourage each child to draw a picture of what he or she liked about the orchard on an index card and glue it to the end of the sentence strip. Punch a hole in the end of each sentence strip and add a single ring binder (buy with office supplies) for a quick and easy book.

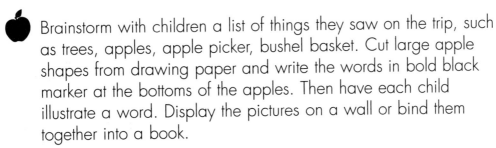

- Brainstorm with children a list of things they saw on the trip, such as trees, apples, apple picker, bushel basket. Cut large apple shapes from drawing paper and write the words in bold black marker at the bottoms of the apples. Then have each child illustrate a word. Display the pictures on a wall or bind them together into a book.

- If you live too far away from an apple orchard, have children make a list of questions they would like to ask and send a dictated letter to an apple grower. Better yet, arrange a conference call with an apple grower and have children ask their own questions. You may wish to rehearse before calling. Call the International Apple Institute (see page 6) for suggested people to call or write.

Visit a packing house that sorts and packages apples for shipping. Take lots of photographs of the trip or have a parent videotape it. When children return to school, see if they can sequence the photos. Encourage children to draw different steps of the process and put them in order on a bulletin board.

Visit a commercial bakery that bakes apple pies or apple cookies, cakes, or turnovers, among other items. The aroma will be worth the trip!

Visit a cider mill to see how apple cider is made or ask someone who works at a mill to demonstrate the process to the class.

See if there is a cannery in your area that processes applesauce or apple pie filling that you can observe.

Take a trip to a fruit stand or farmer's market that has a variety of apples. Have children bring in pennies so you can purchase some apples. Roll the pennies by counting them into stacks of ten and then rolling ten stacks for a dollar. Children may purchase the apple they like the best.

Bring the apples back to school and have children group the apples by variety. Discuss again ways that the varieties of apples are the same and different. Learn the names of the different types of apples. Decide on other ways to sort the apples, such as by color, size, stems and no stems, or shape.

Set up a pretend roadside apple stand. Use a large refrigerator box, turn a rocking boat on its side, or use a play grocery stand or self-supporting puppet theater to make a place for buying and selling apples. Use plastic housekeeping-type apples or wooden or papier mâché apple ornaments that are available in several sizes. Put out a cash register and play money. You will also need brown bags (beg from the grocer) and small baskets (may also be available from a grocer, farmer or apple grower). Have children decide what to call their apple stand and design their own sign. Children may wish to make other signs that tell customers how much everything costs or draw pictures for the apple stand.

PARENT CONNECTION

Invite parents to join the class for an "Apple Experience." They might stay awhile after dropping children off in the morning, come for brunch, or come a few minutes early at dismissal. Or invite parents in for an evening to share the things you have been studying. Consider some of the following ideas.

INVITATIONS

• Have children make apple-shaped invitations inviting parents or special friends to come spend some time with the class.

• You may wish to include the principal or some special staff members on your invitation list.

DECORATING THE ROOM

• Take photographs as you are working through the unit to place around the room. Nothing is a better ice breaker than photographs of children!

• Decorate the room with apple projects the class has completed, such as artwork, big books, and individual books. Use the centerpiece and wreath ideas (see page 44).

DECORATING THE CHILDREN

• Have each child bring in a plain white T-shirt to make an apple T-shirt. Use green and red acrylic paint and real apples cut in half to make prints. Be sure to put pieces of tagboard, newspaper, or brown bag inside the shirts to keep the prints from bleeding through to the back.

• Children may also make apple hats to wear on the special day (see page 42).

 ## REFRESHMENTS

• Have children prepare an apple snack ahead of time, such as apple pie, apples slices dipped in lemon juice, apple chips with caramel fruit dip, caramel apples on a stick, or hot apple cider.

• You may wish to add apple stickers to napkins, plates, and cups for the occasion, or provide paper products with a fall motif.

 ## ENTERTAINMENT

• Have children perform a few apple songs or fingerplays they have learned in this unit.

• Children might also act out a book or song that you have studied.

• Make large cards with one letter on each to spell *A-P-P-L-E* for children to hold while reciting one of the best acrostic poems (*A* is for *apple pie*, *P* is for . . .).

• Consider videotaping the class "performing" and showing the video instead of having children perform live. Or make a video montage of the children working individually or in groups on some of the activities you have been doing in class.

For teachers who are uncomfortable with parents in their classroom:
• Videotape the different things you do in class to create an "Apple Video." At the end of the unit, send the video home for a night with each member of the class. What a wonderful language activity! Children may share all they have learned about apples as their families watch the video with them.

• Be sure to make *several* class big books while working on this unit. As each is complete, have individual children check them out for the night to share with their families.

The main idea is to share with parents something about what their children are learning. It doesn't really matter *how* you share or exactly *what* you share—as long as you offer families an opportunity to get involved with their children's educations.

PUMPKINS

GETTING STARTED

Before you begin, write to:

International Pumpkin Association, Inc.
2155 Union Street
San Francisco, CA 94123
Telephone (415) 346-4447

This organization offers several information sheets about pumpkins for a nominal cost.

Brainstorm with children to find out what they already know about pumpkins and what they would like to know. Begin by making a list of all the things children say they know about pumpkins, correct or incorrect. For example:

Pumpkins are orange.
A pumpkin with a face is called a jack-o'-lantern.
Pumpkin pie is good.

Then make a list of some things they would like to find out.
For example:

What's inside a pumpkin?
How big is the biggest pumpkin?
How many different kinds of pumpkins are there?

Put yourself in the learner role and add some of your own questions to the list. This will help you determine the major concepts you wish to develop and teach. The activities that follow will help you integrate the questions developed by you and the children into your unit.

As you teach this unit, keep a chart of interesting facts about pumpkins. Add a new fact each day. Two sources of interesting information are *In a Pumpkin Shell* by Jennifer Storey Gillis (Storey Communications, 1992) and *The All-Around Pumpkin Book* by Margery Cuyler (Holt, Rinehart, and Winston, 1980).

Here are a few facts to get you started.

- Pumpkins are related to squash and gourds.
- Pumpkins are 90 percent water.
- Most pumpkins weigh 15–30 pounds but can weigh up to 800 pounds!
- Most pumpkins are orange but they can also be yellow or white.
- One cup of fresh cooked pumpkin contains about 49 calories.
- Pumpkin stems are more square than round.
- It takes 3–4 months for a seed to become a pumpkin.
- The squash vine borer is a bug that destroys many pumpkins.
- Pumpkins have yellow flowers.
- Pumpkins have male and female flowers. The pollinated female flowers become pumpkins. The female flower only opens for one day and most of the flowers are male, so very few flowers actually become pumpkins.
- Most pumpkins are grown in Illinois, California, Ohio, and Indiana. Illinois is the number one pumpkin producing state. Eureka, Illinois, is called "The Pumpkin Capital of the World."
- Pumpkins are thought to have originated in North America and were raised by Native American Indians.
- The Pilgrims invented pumpkin pie. They also dried pumpkin shells and made them into bowls for eating.
- There are four types of pumpkins—"cheese" pumpkins grown for eating, "stock" pumpkins grown to feed livestock and make jack-o'-lanterns, "giant" pumpkins, and small "ornamental" pumpkins.
- Pumpkins raised for cooking are sometimes called sugar pumpkins. Popular varieties include Sugar, Small Sugar, and Funny Face. The smaller the pumpkin, the better the flavor.
- Triple Treat seeds produce skinless (hull-less) pumpkin seeds for eating.
- Carved pumpkins last only about four days but uncut pumpkins, kept in a cool place, remain firm for several months.
- Pumpkin Seed Tea was used as medicine in olden days and was thought to kill tapeworms!
- Cinderella rode to the ball in a pumpkin that turned into a royal coach.
- A pumpkinseed fish is a very small, bright orange sunfish. Pumpkinseeds live in North America's freshwater.

LITERATURE CONNECTIONS

 Carve out a pumpkin book nook by adding a bushel basket to your book center filled with books about pumpkins. Ask children in your class and their parents to share books they might have at home, check the library, and go through your classroom library for a collection of "pumpkin" books. You're sure to enjoy some of these stories about pumpkins.

Pumpkin Blanket by Deborah T. Zagwyn (Celestial Arts, 1991). A little girl sacrifices her beloved blanket to save the pumpkins in the garden from frost. Beautiful watercolor illustrations. Can be ordered from the International Pumpkin Association, 2155 Union Street, San Francisco, CA 94123.

The Biggest Pumpkin Ever by Steven Kroll (Holiday House, 1984). A village mouse and a field mouse fall in love with the same pumpkin. One waters the pumpkin by night and the other by day, producing an enormous pumpkin they both enjoy.

Mousekin's Golden House by Edna Miller (Treehouse, 1970). A whitefoot mouse makes a home for the winter in a discarded jack-o'-lantern.

The Pumpkin Patch by Patricia Miles Martin (G. P. Putnam's Sons, 1966). A kindergarten class takes a field trip to a pumpkin patch. Each child chooses a pumpkin to take home except Kate, who finds a pumpkin with a mouse living inside and decides to leave her pumpkin behind.

Pumpkins by M. L. Ray (Harcourt Brace, 1992). Touching story about a special field and a man who wants to save his land. Nice cover picture of pumpkins growing and good illustrations throughout.

The Great Pumpkin Switch by Megan McDonald (Orchard Books, 1992). An old man tells his grandchildren how he and his friend accidentally smashed the pumpkin his sister was growing and how they managed to find a replacement.

Jeb Scarecrow's Pumpkin Patch by Jana Dillon (Houghton Mifflin, 1992). Jeb saves his pumpkin patch from the crows by scaring them with jack-o'-lanterns.

The Vanishing Pumpkin by Tony Johnston (G.P. Putnam's Sons, 1983). A 700-year-old woman and an 800-year-old man discover their pumpkin has been "snitched." After searching a ghoul, a rapscallion, and a varmint, they discover that the wizard has borrowed the pumpkin to make a jack-o'-lantern.

The Wonderful Pumpkin by Lennart Hellsing (Atheneum, 1976). Little Bear and Big Bear plant a seed that becomes a giant pumpkin. The pumpkin grows so large that the bears make it into a house. The wind blows the pumpkin into the ocean and it becomes a houseboat. Later, the bears start a fire and the pumpkin became a blimp. Children will enjoy writing their own bear adventures after they have listened to this story.

The Big, Big Pumpkin by Joan Lezau (Field Publications, 1985). A little bear plants a pumpkin seed by the entrance of his cave. The pumpkin grows so large that it blocks the entrance to the bear's home.

The Berenstain Bears and the Prize Pumpkin by Stan and Jan Berenstain (Random House, 1990). Mama Bear's reminders about the true meaning of Thanksgiving are left in the dust as Papa Bear and the cubs begin a campaign to win first prize in the Thanksgiving Pumpkin Contest.

Peter's Pumpkin House by Colin and Moira Maclean (Kingfisher Books, 1992). This is the delightful story of Peter of pumpkin-eater fame who really is a chimney sweep living in his pumpkin-shell house with his family. They wake up to find that someone, or something, has been nibbling on their house and embark on a quest to solve the identity of the nibbler.

Princess Scargo and the Birthday Pumpkin narrated by Geena Davis (Rabbit Ears Productions, Rowayton, CT, 1992). A beautifully illustrated, 30-minute video from the "American Heroes and Legends" collection. It is the story of a young Indian princess who loves the fish of the sea. For her birthday, a chief from another tribe delivers a huge pumpkin containing all the fish

of the land. When a great drought comes to her land and most of the fish in the ocean die, the little princess decides to give up her wonderful birthday fish. It is said that today the descendants of those same fish swim in Lake Scargo, off Cape Cod.

After sharing some of the stories, encourage children to write stories, dictate stories, and/or draw picture stories about pumpkins. Here are some suggested story starters.

The Biggest Pumpkin Ever
The Pumpkin Smasher
The Great Pumpkin
Mouse's Orange House
The Magic Pumpkin
The Pumpkin Pie Surprise
The Pumpkin Family
Orange Is My Favorite Color
From Seed to Pumpkin
The Pumpkin That Grew and
      Grew

Living in a Pumpkin Shell
The Great Pumpkin Machine
Peter's Pumpkin House
Mystery of the Missing
      Pumpkin
How to Make a Jack-o'-
      Lantern
How to Make a Pumpkin Pie
Eating Pumpkin Pie
I Like Orange

Make a Pumpkin Wall by writing words that children ask about or will use in their writing on small pumpkin-shaped cutouts. Write words such as pumpkin, orange, seeds, stem, vine, leaves, stringy, big, fat, plump, and round.

Play Pumpkin Wall Bingo using the pumpkin-related words from the previous activity. Have children copy down five words of their choice from the Pumpkin Wall on sheets of paper (or use laminated orange pumpkin shapes and washable markers). Call words from the wall at random and have children cross out the words you name. The first child to strike through all his or her words yells, "Pumpkin!" Repeat the game with new sets of words.

When you have accumulated many words, have children create a picture graph by sorting the words by initial letters. Take the words off the wall with tape still attached and distribute. Write the letters of the alphabet across the bottom of the chalkboard and have children place the words from the wall above the appropriate initial letter, working from the bottom up. When all the words have been sorted, discuss which letter has the most words, the least number of words, no words at all, and so on.

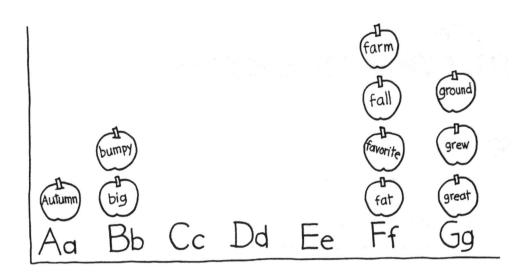

Make a large pumpkin-shaped journal for each child. Cut two orange construction-paper pumpkin shapes for the front and back covers of the journals (cut on the fold to join front and back) or use large sheets from a pumpkin-shaped notepad—one for each cover. Cut writing paper the same shape for children's pictures and words. Or, for easier journals, staple plain sheets of white paper together and have children draw pumpkins on the "cover." Encourage children to use drawings, words, and sentences with invented, temporary spelling in their journals.

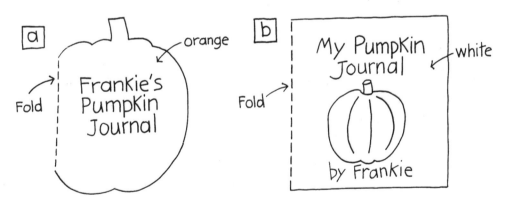

RHYTHM 'N RHYME

Teach the nursery rhyme "Peter, Peter, Pumpkin Eater."

Peter, Peter, Pumpkin Eater
Had a wife and couldn't keep her,
Put her in a pumpkin shell
And there he kept her very well.

Encourage children to memorize the traditional rhyme. Give each child a small treat such as a pumpkin drawn on the back of the hand, a piece of pumpkin-shaped candy, or a pumpkin sticker, when they have recited the verse successfully.

Invite children to illustrate Peter, his wife, and the pumpkin house with tempera, watercolors, crayons, or markers.

Write the nursery rhyme on chart paper and point to each word with a pumpkin pointer as you read to reinforce left-to-right progression. You can make a pumpkin pointer by hot gluing a small three-dimensional pumpkin to the end of a dowel, or a construction paper or fun foam pumpkin to a ruler. Add some curling green ribbon tendrils.

Write the entire rhyme on sentence strips and have children watch while you cut the strips into individual words. Place the words in order in a pocket chart and read the rhyme with the class. Ask children to close their eyes and choose a child to come up and turn one word backwards. Children open their eyes and try to guess the mystery word. Whoever guesses the word takes the next turn.

After you have cut the rhyme into individual words, distribute the word cards to children. Display the rhyme on chart paper and ask children to form each line of the rhyme (one at a time) by coming up and holding their words in front of them. Help children stand in a line facing the rest of the class, so they are in same order as the verse. Read the line they have formed as a class. Those children may then sit down to make way for the children who will form the next line of the verse.

 Look for Joan Walsh Anglund's *In a Pumpkin Shell* (Harcourt Brace Jovanovich, 1969), which contains an illustrated nursery rhyme for each letter of the alphabet. "Peter, Peter, Pumpkin Eater" is written and illustrated for the letter *P*. Display each rhyme as you read the poems, encouraging children to identify the letters of the alphabet and guess the words from the illustrations. Make a class Pumpkin Alphabet Book by having children brainstorm pumpkin-related words for each letter. Try some of the following if you get stuck.

angry pumpkin faces
bumpy pumpkin, (pumpkin) bread
candle, Cinderella's carriage, canned pumpkin
delicious pie!
excellent pie/cookies/muffins!
fall, farm, fruit
"gunky" (inside of the pumpkin),
Halloween jack-o'-lanterns, happy faces
Indians (planted), Illinois (top-producing state)
jack-o'-lantern
kitchen (cooking pies!)
lantern (how jack-o'-lanterns were first used)
miniature pumpkins, muffins (pumpkin)
nutritious
orange
pumpkin pie, pumpkin patch
quick-growing—NOT!
round pumpkin
seeds, stem, scarecrow (pumpkin head)

Thanksgiving
ugly jack-o'-lantern face
vines
weeds (to pull), water
x-tra good pie!
yellow blossoms
z-z-z-z (sleeping jack-o'-lantern)

Write the words on sheets of drawing paper and have volunteers illustrate each word with colored pencils, markers, crayons, or paint. Put the pictures in alphabetical order, add a cover, and bind together for a class book.

Children will enjoy reading *Peter's Pumpkin House* by Colin and Moira Maclean (Kingfisher Books, 1992). This is the story of Peter of pumpkin-eater fame who really is a chimney sweep living in a pumpkin-shell house with his wife and baby. They wake up one morning to find that someone, or something, has been nibbling on their house. As Peter searches the city for the culprit, he finds nursery rhyme characters using pumpkins in many different ways. Finally, Peter discovers that it's really a goat from Shoe Cottage nibbling away each night. The old lady who lives in the shoe is so upset that she gives Peter a magic pumpkin seed that before long has grown into a new pumpkin house.

Encourage children to make up couplets using their own names. Before starting, brainstorm with children words that end with *-er*. For example,

Kyra, Kyra, pumpkin eater
Is so smart and not a cheater.

Marco, Marco, pumpkin eater
Was a boy and a fine leader.

Nadine, Nadine, pumpkin eater
Had a mom who'd always feed her.

Willy, Willy, pumpkin hater
Hated pie, liked apples better.

These couplets might be a take-home project for children to create and illustrate with their families on large pieces of tagboard cut into pumpkin shapes. Display the finished projects for all to see.

🍎 Make a class book entitled *In a Pumpkin Shell*. Have each child cut a pumpkin with a window from orange construction paper. Glue the pumpkins to white construction paper pages. Inside the pumpkin window, children may draw a picture of who they would keep in a pumpkin shell. Add the words, "(Child's name) would keep _____ in a pumpkin shell." Display the pictures on a bulletin board and then bind them together into a class big book, adding a cover of self-portraits and a title page.

🍎 Sing these words to the tune of "Way Down Yonder in the Paw Paw Patch."

Where, oh where is dear little _____ ?
(repeat twice more)
Way down yonder in the pumpkin patch.

Come on, boys *(girls)*, let's go find him *(her)*,
(Repeat twice more)
Way down yonder in the pumpkin patch.

Pickin' up pumpkins, put 'em in a basket.
(Repeat twice more)
Way down yonder in the pumpkin patch.

 Take turns using different names in the first verse. In the second verse, have boys sing, "Come on, boys . . ." and then girls sing, "Come on, girls . . . ." The last verse may be acted out by everyone.

Make a big book to represent the song by having children draw or paint pictures of themselves in a pumpkin patch. Under each picture, write "(child's name) is picking up pumpkins." Bind the pages together and add a cover.

 Teach these original words by Kristen VanValkenburg to the tune of "The Farmer in the Dell."

I see a pumpkin.
Oh, I see a pumpkin.
Heigh-ho! Fall is here!
I see a pumpkin.

Choose one big and round.
Oh, choose one big and round.
Heigh-ho! Fall is here!
Choose one big and round.

Choose one short and fat . . .
Choose one tall and thin . . .
Choose one really bumpy . . .

Feel free to make up other verses with children and close with the following verse.

> Let's take them home.
> Oh, let's take them home.
> Heigh-ho! Fall is here!
> Let's take them home.

Write the words for each verse on white drawing paper and have volunteers illustrate each one. Display the illustrated verses on a bulletin board and then bind into a pumpkin big book entitled *I See a Pumpkin!*

I see a pumpkin.

Choose one big and round.

Choose one short and fat.

LETTERS, LANGUAGE, AND PHONICS

Challenge children to think! Place a pumpkin of any size on a table and have children try to name the following. You can probably think of lots more.

Another fruit that is orange.
A vegetable that is orange.
An animal that eats pumpkins.
Something bigger than this pumpkin.
Something smaller than this pumpkin.
Something about the same size as this pumpkin.
Something that would break if you threw this pumpkin at it.
Something that is heavier than this pumpkin.
Something that is lighter than this pumpkin.
Something that weighs about the same as this pumpkin.
Something harder than this pumpkin.
Something softer than this pumpkin.
Something that you could balance on this pumpkin.

Make pumpkin-shaped alphabet flash cards. Write uppercase letters on tagboard pumpkin shapes or use sheets from pumpkin-shaped notepads—one letter on each pumpkin. Use these flash cards with small groups of children and leave the pumpkins out to encourage individual children to put them in alphabetical order. When children are proficient with uppercase letters, make a set of lowercase letters. For more mature children, flash the cards and challenge children to tell what letter comes next or supply a word that starts with that letter.

Cut pumpkin shapes from construction paper or tagboard to make a pumpkin game. Cut each pumpkin in half so that only the matches will fit back together (for a more difficult game, make all the cuts identical). On one half, write uppercase letters and on the other, write lowercase. Children put the pumpkins together by matching upper and lowercase letters. More mature children can match alphabet letters to initial and final consonant sounds, rhyming words, and so on.

 Write the upper or lowercase letters of the alphabet on a long sentence strip with orange crayon. Invite children to use their index fingers to trace over each letter as they say it aloud. The waxy crayon will give tactile reinforcement. Then give children small brushes and orange tempera paint or watercolor and have them paint over each letter. (To keep children from using other colors in a watercolor palette, put a strip of masking tape over all except orange or pop out the orange and put it in a baby food jar lid.) More mature children can paint the alphabet without a model or paint sight or spelling words.

 Make a Pumpkin Alphabet Game to play like bingo. Cut orange pumpkin shapes from tagboard and write four to eight letters of the alphabet on each pumpkin (lowercase letters on one side and uppercase on the other). Call the letters at random. Less mature children may need to see flash cards in order to match the letters. Use small pumpkin-shaped erasers, orange bingo chips, orange pompoms or pumpkin-shaped candies for markers. More mature children can play using sight word vocabulary, color words, number words, or spelling words instead of the alphabet.

Write the letter *P* on a piece of chart paper, orange kraft paper cut in the shape of a pumpkin, or a commercially made pumpkin chart. Challenge children to brainstorm all the words that they can think of that start with the letter *P*. Add to the list as the week goes along. For more mature children, write the letters *P-U-M-P-K-I-N* across the top of the chalkboard and have children list words under each letter that begin with that letter. For the second *P*, children should use different words from their first *P* list! Divide the most mature children into small cooperative groups and see how many words they can make using the letters of the word *PUMPKIN*, (*in*, *pin*, *kin*, *pun*, *pump*, and so on).

Use the list of words from the previous activity to write an acrostic poem on the word *pumpkin*. Write the word down the left side of a sheet of chart paper. Divide the class into small cooperative groups, have children work individually, or work with the class as a whole to write poems.

Perfect pumpkins
Unusually round
Mostly orange
Pumpkin pie
Keep it warm!
In my mouth
None left!

Cut large pumpkin shapes and add pictures of categories to each card—for example, spoons, nuts, things to write with, or things that go. Collect real items for each category. For spoons, you might use a plastic spoon, teaspoon, measuring spoon, serving spoon, slotted spoon, and baby spoon. For nuts, you might collect a plastic nut from an artificial arrangement, a real walnut, pecan, peanut, and Brazil nut. Put all the items into one container (a plastic trick-or-treat pumpkin is appropriate) and have children sort the items into correct pumpkin categories.

Discuss pumpkin varieties and characteristics with children. New pumpkin varieties are developed and grown each year. Divide the class into groups of three or four and have each group come up with a new pumpkin variety and list of characteristics. Encourage them to draw a picture of their new pumpkin. Here is a list of some popular varieties.

Big Max	Often exceeds 200 lbs. per pumpkin
Prizewinner	May reach 400 lbs.
Triple Treat	Looks good, tastes good, and has hull-less seeds
Cinderella	Original, deep flame pumpkin
Lumina	White, creamy pumpkin
Sugar	Sweet, best for cooking
Bushkin	Short, bushy vines
Jack-Be-Little	Miniature
Munchkin	Miniature
Jack-Be-Quick	Shorter growing time
Baby Boo	White Jack-Be-Quick

Help children practice classifying by making several baskets with category names such as clothing, furniture, animals, things to read, and people (use picture clues if necessary). Cut pumpkin shapes and put one picture on each pumpkin. Children may put out the baskets (basket shapes can be flat or glued to the fronts of individual milk cartons) and put the appropriate pumpkins into each basket.

Pumpkins are sometimes referred to as a squash and are related to the gourd family. Bring in an assortment of yellow crookneck squash, zucchini, pattypan, acorn squash, gourds, and small pumpkins. Cut one of each apart and ask children if they see any characteristics in common. Encourage children to sort them by type, color, and size, or to order them from smallest to largest.

Encourage children to set up a fruit and vegetable stand with their squash, gourds, and pumpkins by adding small baskets or bags, a self-supporting puppet stand with a homemade sign, a play cash register, pretend money, a postage or food scale, and any other items they wish. Children may take turns pretending to be customers and sellers.

Put one of the pumpkin family vegetables behind your back and describe it to the class. See if they can identify which one you are describing. Or put all in front of the children and describe one. Children may guess which one you are describing. More mature children may take turns describing the vegetables for their peers.

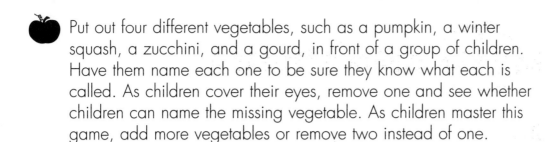 Put out four different vegetables, such as a pumpkin, a winter squash, a zucchini, and a gourd, in front of a group of children. Have them name each one to be sure they know what each is called. As children cover their eyes, remove one and see whether children can name the missing vegetable. As children master this game, add more vegetables or remove two instead of one.

Brainstorm with children a list of words that rhyme (or almost rhyme) with pumpkin, such as *jump in, bumpkin, somethin'*, or *come in*. Encourage children to add nonsense words, such as *flumpkin* or *grumpkin*. (Children will have to tell you what their words mean!) Then write a class poem using the words from your list. You may wish to have volunteers illustrate each line of the poem for a big book.

MATH AND SCIENCE

 Teach the following traditional fingerplay to your class.

> 5 little pumpkins sitting on the gate.
> The first one said, "Oh my, it's getting late!"
> The second one said, "There's a storm in the air."
> The third one said, "I don't really care!"
> The fourth one said, "Let's run and run and run."
> The fifth one said, "Oh, this is fun!"
> Whoo-o-o-o-o went the wind
> And out went the lights
> And the 5 little pumpkins rolled out of sight.

Cut five orange felt pumpkins for your flannelboard. Repeat the fingerplay while you manipulate the pumpkins. Leave the pumpkins out so children may manipulate them later as they practice the poem.

Make a pumpkin mitt to illustrate the rhyme by gluing a piece of Velcro to each finger of a garden glove. Use large orange pompoms for pumpkins, gluing a small piece of a green or brown pipe cleaner or felt to each pompom for a stem. Glue matching pieces of Velcro to the back of each "pumpkin." As you recite the rhyme, stick a pumpkin onto each finger to illustrate each number. Close your fist and roll your hand behind your back for the last verse.

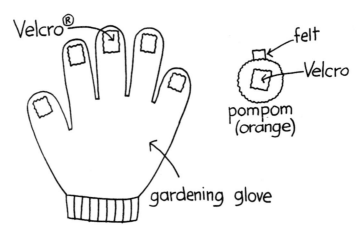

Use the big book *Five Little Pumpkins* by Sheila Somerville (Nellie Edge Resources, 1988) or the small board book that is packaged with a small stuffed pumpkin, *My Little Treat: Five Little Pumpkins* illustrated by James Young (Harper Festival, 1995) that illustrate variations of the rhyme. Both versions read, ". . . The second one said, "There's a witch in the air. . . ."

Cut five large pumpkins from orange tagboard. Cut a circle in the middle for a child's face to peer through and invite five children to act out the poem. Encourage them to memorize the words their pumpkins say. Read the poem, stopping to let children say their lines. Continue with a new set of five until each child has had a turn.

Make a class big book based on the rhyme. Have each child draw a pumpkin with marker or crayon. Cut out each pumpkin drawing. Make the gates by having children tear or cut gray or light brown construction paper into strips. Glue the strips into a fence design on dark blue construction paper (use black paper for "Whoo-o-o-o went the wind and out went the lights!") Write the words of each line on the bottoms of the pages and place the appropriate number of pumpkins on the gates. (Just an empty gate for "And the 5 little pumpkins rolled out of sight.") Extra pumpkins? Place them on the cover.

Collect tongue depressors and tiny pumpkin stickers. Write a number from 1 to 10 on each tongue depressor. To keep the stickers from coming off, paint over them with clear nail polish or spray with clear acrylic. Place the appropriate number of pumpkin stickers on each tongue depressor and have children order the sticks numerically. For a variation, use stickers without numerals. Children may match the sticks to a chart with the numbers.

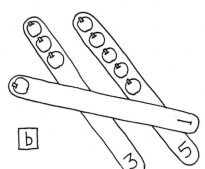

Make dot-to-dot pumpkins using numbers your children know. Write a number by each dot and have children connect the dots with orange crayons or markers. They can finish the pumpkins by coloring them and adding details if they wish. Leave out orange markers and blank white drawing paper to encourage children to make dot-to-dot pumpkins for each other.

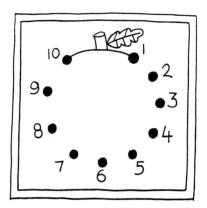

Help children practice writing numbers and sets. Write numbers down the left side of a sheet of paper (larger numbers for more mature children). Have each child use an orange bingo dabber, pumpkin rubber stamp, or a cork or fingerprint with a (washable) orange stamp pad to stamp the appropriate number of pumpkins beside each number. To provide daily practice, write numbers down the side of a sheet of paper and have children use manipulatives, such as orange bingo chips or pumpkin-shaped erasers, for counting.

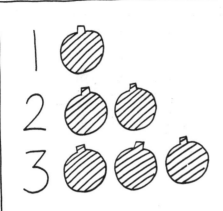

 Practice counting with this version of "Ten Little Indians."

1 little, 2 little, 3 little pumpkins,
4 little, 5 little, 6 little pumpkins,
7 little, 8 little, 9 little pumpkins,
10 little pumpkins on a vine.

Have each child paint a paper plate orange (or use orange paper plates), add stem and leaves, and staple to a tongue depressor or craft stick. Choose ten children to stand up front with their pumpkins, holding up their pumpkins when their numbers are sung. Another way to practice the song is to have ten children stand up, one at a time, as you touch them on their heads, and then sit down as you touch them on their heads again counting backwards.

As children are learning the song, cut ten pumpkins from orange felt for your flannelboard to use as you sing. Later add flannel numbers. Leave the flannel pumpkins and numbers out for children to order.

Write the numbers 1 to 10 on each child's fingernails, one number per nail, with a washable marker. Be sure to write the numbers so they are "right-side up" when the child reads them left to right. Have children hold up the appropriate number as you sing it.

Make a book to illustrate the song. Cut pumpkin shapes from orange construction paper or have children draw, color, and cut out enough pumpkins to illustrate each line of the song. Write the words for each number and place the appropriate number of pumpkins on a page. Add a cover and title page and bind together into a book.

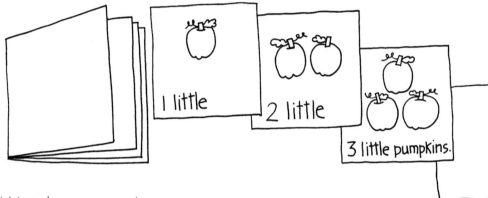

Write the song on chart paper. Provide pumpkin-shaped sticky notes with one number word on each note. Children may place the sticky notes over their corresponding numerals on the chart.

Photograph the children illustrating the numbers 1 to 10. Use pumpkin-shaped face frames, pumpkin paper plates, or have each child hold a real pumpkin. In the first picture, have one child with one pumpkin. In the next picture, have two children holding or dressed as two pumpkins, and so on up to ten children and ten pumpkins. Laminate so children may order the pictures numerically. For more mature children, make +, −, and = signs and challenge children to use the photographs to create simple addition and subtraction problems with sums less than 10.

Play Number Bingo with pumpkin shapes. Cut grids for four to eight numbers from white paper and place on orange tagboard pumpkins. Write a different series of numbers on each pumpkin. Be sure they are numbers you have studied. Call out numbers in random order (less mature children may need number flash cards held up as you call each number for visual reinforcement). You can use candy pumpkins as markers (be prepared for the child who keeps eating his markers!), orange bingo chips, or pumpkin-shaped erasers. The first child to fill the card wins. More mature children may use the numbers on the cards as answers to simple addition and subtraction problems (you call 4 + 1; child marks 5) or you may hold up number words and have children match the numerals on their cards.

 Use pumpkin-shaped erasers or candy, orange bingo chips, or small orange pompoms as counters. Write the numbers 1 to 10 or higher in a line across the top of a plastic laminate table with permanent marker.

5	2	8	4	1	3

Add vertical lines between the numbers to make columns. Put the counters in a plastic pumpkin so children may count out the appropriate number of pumpkins under each number. Permanent marker will erase with hair spray or alcohol.

 Make construction paper numbers 1 to 10 or higher using stencils or die-cuts. Give each child a set of numbers to glue in order on a strip of paper. Children may use an orange bingo dabber, fingerprint, or cork with a (washable) orange ink pad to place the appropriate number of "pumpkins" on each number (one pumpkin on the number 1 and so on).

Ask each child to bring in one of the miniature pumpkins available in the fall. When you have about a dozen, decide on a number and have small groups of children divide all the pumpkins by sets. For example, "Put all the pumpkins in sets of three." Ask children to decide on other ways they can sort the little pumpkins, such as by size, stems or no stems, and so on. Have the children order the pumpkins from smallest to largest, and decide which is the tallest, shortest, fattest, and thinnest.

Have children use a balance scale to weigh the pumpkins. See if they can find two pumpkins that weigh the same. Ask children to decide which pumpkin is the lightest and which is the heaviest by weighing them. Encourage children to order the pumpkins from heaviest to lightest.

Put out three small pumpkins labeled A, B, C. Let the children use teddy bear counters (or other measures such as pumpkin-shaped candies or pennies) and see how many it takes to balance each of the pumpkins.

Help children use a pumpkin Venn diagram to compare a pumpkin with an orange, a basketball, or another piece of fruit, such as an apple or pear. In the left section, write things that describe only the pumpkin. In the right section, write things that describe only the orange. Where the circles intersect, write things the two have in common.

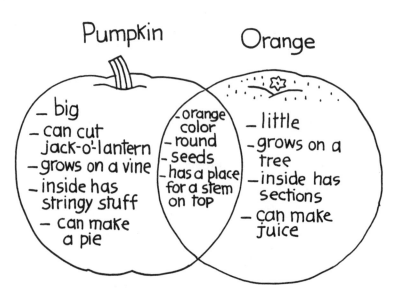

Bring in a large pumpkin, ask a parent to volunteer to supply one, or take the class to pick one. After you have your pumpkin, invite each child to cut a piece of string or yarn that he or she thinks is exactly the length that will fit around the pumpkin at its widest point (circumference). After all children have cut pieces, have them see how their strings fit. Cut a piece that is the exact circumference (in a different color from those the children have cut) and have children hold up their strings beside yours. Ask the class whether each string is longer or shorter than the exact measure. Have children decide who made the best estimate. Order the strings from shortest to longest.

Before cutting your pumpkin, have children guess how many seeds are inside. Give each child a pumpkin-shaped piece of paper or sticky note on which to guess. Count the seeds after they have dried. You may want to put seeds in lines of 5 or 10 if there are many. Compare estimates with the actual number of seeds.

Save the seeds from your class pumpkin. Put them in a colander and drain, picking out all the other gunk. Leave the seeds to dry on a cookie sheet or waxed paper. Make a number-set game with seeds as counters by cutting pumpkins from orange construction paper or tagboard. Write a number on each paper pumpkin and have children count the correct number of seeds onto each cutout. If you plan to cook the seeds, use dried lima beans to represent the seeds or buy packages of pumpkin seeds for planting.

Cut your pumpkin in a dry sand or water table. Children may pull out the seeds and gunk and put it right in the table to play with. Carve the eyes, nose, and mouth and leave the discards in the table with small pumpkin knives made especially for children. Leave all the remains in the table for the day, adding about an inch of water so children may enjoy active exploration. Add strainer, colanders, bowls, and other appropriate items. Encourage children to separate the seeds into a colander later in the day.

Discuss with children how a pumpkin grows.

Pumpkin seeds are planted in the ground.
Rain and sunshine help the seed to grow.
The seed sprouts and grows into a vine.
The vine bears yellow flowers.
Flowers turn into small green pumpkins.
Pumpkins grow larger and turn orange.

The growth of a pumpkin is a popular sequencing task, so look for cut-and-paste dittos or sequencing puzzles that illustrate the growth of a pumpkin to use with your class.

🍎 Teach children this song to the tune of "The Farmer in the Dell."

The farmer plants the seeds.
The farmer plants the seeds.
Heigh ho! The pumpkin-o!
The farmer plants the seeds.

The rain begins to fall . . .
The sun begins to shine . . .
The seed begins to sprout . . .
The vine has yellow flowers . . .
Flowers make green pumpkins . . .
Pumpkins then turn orange . . .
And now the harvest's in . . .

Write the words to the song on chart paper and use a pumpkin pointer to follow the words from left to right as you sing them. Leave the pumpkin pointer out so children can come up and "read" the song by themselves.

Have children illustrate each verse of the song. Place their pictures on pumpkin-shaped sheets of orange construction paper or tagboard. Then tape the pictures in order to make accordion books or make one big class book by having volunteers illustrate each verse.

🍎 Be sure to read the simple and beautifully illustrated tale *Pumpkin Pumpkin* by Jeanne Titherington (Greenwillow Books, 1986). Jamie plants pumpkin seeds in the spring. All summer he watches his pumpkin grow from a tiny sprout to a huge orange pumpkin. By Halloween, it is ready to pick and carve into a jack-o'-lantern. But best of all, inside the pumpkin are seeds to be planted next spring. This book is a celebration of life for the very youngest.

Have children study each double-page spread and draw their own versions, substituting a picture of themselves for Jamie. Place each picture on a paper plate with the words from the book underneath. Arrange the pictures in a circle, so children can see that this is a circle story beginning and ending with seeds.

 Here are some other books about pumpkin growing to have on hand to read to children.

The Little Pumpkin Book by Katherine Ross (Random House, 1992).
Two children plant pumpkin seeds, watch them grow, and then make jack-o'-lanterns, pumpkin cookies, and pumpkin pie. A chunky shape book for the youngest child.

The Pumpkin Patch Parable by Liz Curtis Higgs (Thomas Nelson, 1995).
A charming story for young readers that illustrates how a loving farmer turns a simple pumpkin into a glorious sight. This version includes biblical references in small print.

It's Pumpkin Time! by Zoe Hall (Blue Sky Press, 1994).
Simple text and colorful pictures provide a perfect description of the growing pumpkin from seed to jack-o'-lantern. Ends with a night of trick-or-treating on Halloween.

Growing Pumpkins by Melvin Berger (Newbridge Communications, 1993).
Part of the "Early Science Series" in big-book format and extremely useful for teaching the pumpkin-growing sequence. Simple text and colorful photographs. Excellent teacher's guide included.

The Pumpkin People by David and Maggie Cavagnaro (Charles Scribner's Sons, 1979).
An engaging circle story that begins and ends with a pumpkin seed.

From Seed to Jack-o'-lantern by Hannah Lyons-Johnson (Lothrop, 1974)
Black-and-white photographs of the life of a pumpkin from seed to jack-o'-lantern. Explains pollination and fertilization in simple terms. Instructions for planting your own pumpkin, inside or out, and other useful information.

Pumpkin Patch by Elizabeth King (Dutton Children's Books, 1990). Text and color photography describe the activities in a pumpkin patch as seeds become fat pumpkins ready to be carved into jack-o'-lanterns.

In a Pumpkin Shell by Jennifer Storey Gillis (Storey Communications, 1992).
Detailed information for the beginner on saving or choosing pumpkin seeds, care of the crop, harvesting and storing, creating unique pumpkins, and producing prize-winning pumpkins. Also includes some art activities and recipes.

Children will love watching pumpkin vines grow. To be ready in October, seeds should be planted in May, as pumpkins take from 90 to 120 days to mature. Save your seeds and think about having this year's class plant the seeds as a gift for next year's class. A fall surprise! Before committing to pumpkin planting, check with your local State University Cooperative Extension, which can put you in touch with agricultural specialists—your county agents. You'll need to know how pumpkins grow in your area and someone to call for help.

Follow the information in the books listed previously to plant your own pumpkin seeds. *In a Pumpkin Shell* (or the older *The All-Around Pumpkin Book* by Margery Cuyler, Holt, Rinehart, and Winston, 1980) tells how to save seeds and gives easy-to-follow directions on what you need and how to plant. Or order "A Guide to Growing Pumpkins for the Home Gardener" from the International Pumpkin Association, Inc., (2155 Union Street, San Francisco, CA 94123, 415–346–4447) at a nominal cost.

Look for *My First Garden: Pumpkins* by Derek and Sandra Rangecroft.

An alternative to growing pumpkins is to have children watch pumpkin seeds sprout. This can be done by planting a couple of seeds in small paper cups. Or give each child a plastic zipper bag containing two damp paper towels and three pumpkin seeds (either save and dry seeds from cutting your own pumpkin or use packaged seeds). Hang the bags, so children may watch them sprout (takes a few days). Children can easily observe the plant parts through the plastic bags. Encourage them to examine the sprouts each day and label the parts (seed, roots, stem, leaves).

Pumpkin seeds can be ordered from

W. Atlee Burpee and Co.
300 Park Avenue
Warminster, Pennsylvania 18991–0001
1–800–888–1447

As Grown Seed Company
7000 Portage Rd.
Kalamazoo, Michigan 49001
1–616–323–4000

Burrell Seed Company
P.O. Box 150
Rocky Ford, Colorado 81067
1–719–254–3318

Comstock, Ferre & Company
236 Main Street
Wethersfield, Connecticut 06109
1–203–529–3319

G.W. Park Seed Company
Cokesbury Road
Greenwood, South Carolina 29649
1–800–845–3369

Or write the **International Pumpkin Association, Inc.**
(2155 Union Street, San Francisco, CA 94123) for a complete
list of seed companies.

COOKING

Make toasted pumpkin seeds with children. After you have made them, have children write a "How to . . ." story with you. Start sentences with the words *first, next, and then,* and *finally.*

Toasted Pumpkin Seeds

pumpkin seeds from real pumpkin (about 1 cup)
1 tsp. Worcestershire sauce
3 Tbs. melted butter or margarine
1 tsp. salt

Remove all pulp from seeds and place in a colander. Rinse with cold water. Boil seeds in salted water for 10 minutes or steam for 30 minutes. Drain, pat dry with a paper towel, and allow to dry on a cookie sheet. Mix Worcestershire sauce, butter or margarine, and salt in a bowl and add the pumpkin seeds, stirring until well coated. Spread seeds on a baking sheet. Bake at 225°F for 1–2 hours, watching for burning. Cool and enjoy.

Turn a pumpkin into pumpkin bread, pumpkin pie, or pumpkin mush. A small pumpkin will provide enough for a small pie or some pumpkin bread. You cannot use a jack-o'-lantern that you have allowed to dry inside for even a short time—you need a new pumpkin for this project. Ask at the store for a *sugar pumpkin*—a variety grown especially for cooking. Cut the pumpkin in half and have children pull out all the gunky stuff (seeds and strings) with their hands. This will be their favorite part! Use a blunt knife or large spoon to scrape the rest of the strings out. Cut the pumpkin into large chunks and *steam* (place chunks in a metal colander or steamer over 1–2 inches of water) on medium high for about 45 minutes or bake at 350°F for about 30 minutes. It is done when the meat is soft and the peel turns brown and starts to come off. Cool and remove peel. Place the pumpkin meat in a blender or food processor and purée. Now it's ready for a pie or bread. If you want the children to taste the plain pumpkin, try the following recipe.

Pumpkin Mush

1 cup pumpkin
1/4 cup honey
1/4 tsp. cinnamon
1/4 tsp. nutmeg

Mash together and enjoy!

Write a fact book about making pumpkin mush.
On Page 1, include facts about the pumpkin before it was cut.
On Page 2, include facts about the cutting of the pumpkin
  and gunk removal.
On Page 3, include facts about mashing the pumpkin and
  spices together.
On Page 4, include facts about eating the pumpkin!
Make a cover by having each child draw and cut out a pumpkin.
Glue on the cover collage style.

 Try these muffins for a snack that's sure to be a hit.

Yummy Pumpkin Muffins

2 cups all-purpose flour
2 cups sugar
1 tsp. soda
2 tsp. baking powder
3 tsp. pumpkin pie spice *or* 1 tsp. each cinnamon, nutmeg, cloves
1/2 tsp. salt
1 cup oil
15 oz. can of pumpkin *or* 1 cup real pumpkin
4 eggs
1/2 cup chopped nuts and/or 1/2 cup raisins (optional)

Preheat oven to 350°F. Use muffin liners or spray-on cooking oil
for easy muffin removal. Blend all ingredients in bowl and mix at
low speed until moistened. Beat at medium speed for two more
minutes. Fill muffin liners about three-quarters full and bake 20–25
minutes. Makes 2–3 dozen regular-sized muffins. Muffins can be
iced with cream cheese icing if desired. Serve with apple juice
and popcorn for a special seasonal treat.

 Americans make approximately 88 million pumpkin pies using canned pumpkin every Thanksgiving! Treat your class to a pumpkin pie. Pop any of the many brands of frozen pies into the oven or make a pie with the class. Buy a prepared 9-inch unbaked crust and follow package directions. Use the following recipe for the filling.

Pumpkin Pie

2 slightly beaten eggs
1-1/2 cans pumpkin or 1-1/2 cups fresh pumpkin
1 cup sugar or 1/2 cup each molasses and brown sugar
1/2 tsp. salt
1 tsp. cinnamon, 1/4 tsp. each ginger, cloves, nutmeg, allspice
   or 2 tsp. pumpkin pie spice
1-2/3 cups evaporated milk
1 tsp. vanilla

Combine eggs, pumpkin, sugar, vanilla, salt, and spices. Gradually add evaporated milk. Mix well and pour into unbaked shell. Bake for 50–60 minutes at 400°F or until a toothpick inserted into the pie comes out clean. Let cool before cutting. For individual pies, use muffin tins and a flattened muffin liner as a pattern to cut circles from the pie crust. Spray the muffin tins with cooking oil, place the crusts in each cup, and fill with pumpkin pie filling. Reduce cooking time. Cool and serve with whipped cream or make a crumbly topping by mixing together pecan pieces, brown sugar, a little flour, and melted butter.

 Try one of the pumpkin recipes from *In a Pumpkin Shell* by Jennifer Storey Gillis (Storey Communications, 1992) for concoctions such as Pumpkin Soup, Fried Pumpkin Flowers, Pumpkin Snack Chips, or Pumpkin Waffles. Order "A Guide to Selecting, Cooking & Storing Pumpkins" from the International Pumpkin Association (see page 50) for Pumpkin Soup, Stuffed Sugar Pumpkin, or Pumpkin Cobbler, or look for *The New Pumpkin Book* by Terry Pimsleur and Mary Bettencourt for other interesting recipes.

Look for seasonal snacks such as individually wrapped pumpkin pies and other special pumpkin treats marketed around Halloween and Thanksgiving. Any of these will give children the flavor of pumpkin.

After the children have had a variety of experiences touching, feeling, and tasting pumpkins, have each child fill in the blanks for a Five Senses Poem about pumpkins or pumpkin pie. Write each dictated poem on pumpkin-shaped orange construction paper. You may wish to have parent volunteers or older children help with the dictation.

Pumpkins smell _____ .

Pumpkins look _____ .

Pumpkins feel _____ .

Pumpkins sound _____ .

Pumpkins taste _____ .

MANIPULATIVES

Put orange food coloring in your water table or tub. Tell children you are going to put a few drops of red and a few drops of yellow in the water and let them predict what will happen. Add the drops and encourage children to stir the water. If you do not have a see-through table, add clear plastic containers for measuring and pouring.

Ask children whether they think pumpkins will float or sink. Try several small pumpkins and then larger ones if you have a lot of water in the table (they float). Cut the pumpkin apart and ask children whether they think pumpkin *pieces* will float or sink. Then ask about seeds. Provide a few pumpkin chunks and some seeds for the children to manipulate in the water table for a day.

Cut a small pumpkin in half and leave in the water table for the day with about two inches of water for a sensory experience. Add some spoons, plastic knives, and pumpkin knives made especially for young children so they may cut the pumpkin, explore the seeds, "stringy stuff," the inside, and outside of pumpkins.

With the children's help, make orange play dough using the following recipe.

2 cups flour
1 cup salt
2 cups water
orange food coloring/paste added to water
2 Tbs. vegetable oil
4 tsp. cream of tartar

Mix all ingredients and cook over medium heat. Play dough is done when it pulls easily away from the sides of the pot.

Or make a batch of yellow and a batch of red, so children may "discover" orange by mixing the two. Add some pumpkin seeds to the play dough area for children to use as decorations and for making jack-o'-lantern faces.

Look for pumpkin and jack-o'-lantern cookie cutters in different sizes to use with the play dough. Encourage children to make pumpkins by cutting them with cookie cutters and by rolling balls of play dough.

Make orange sand in your sand table. Add orange food coloring/paste (red and yellow) to a bottle of rubbing alcohol. Pour the colored alcohol over your sand and mix well with a large shovel or spoon, or with your hands (wear rubber gloves—the alcohol will stain). The orange sand will be dry by the end of the day.

Place orange markers and crayons at the writing table along with commercial or homemade pumpkin stencils. Make your own stencils by cutting pumpkin shapes into the tops of large plastic lids from margarine tubs or coffee cans. Show children how to place the lids flat on drawing paper and trace the pumpkin shapes inside.

Make pumpkin sewing cards from large, pumpkin-shaped notepad sheets glued to tagboard and laminated. Or cut pumpkin shapes from orange tagboard. Punch holes around the perimeter. Children may use shoelaces to string the cards. Often you can find seasonal laces printed with pumpkins.

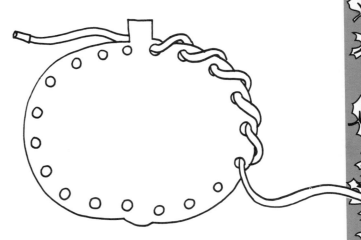

Turn the overhead projector into a center. Make a transparency of two or three simple pumpkin drawings. Place the projector on the floor and provide white paper and markers. Project the picture of the pumpkins on a wall. You may wish to cover the wall area with a large sheet of bulletin board paper, so stray marks will not get on the wall or project the picture on a chalkboard and have children use colored chalk. Show children how to hold or tape their papers so they can trace around the pumpkins on the wall to make their own pumpkin pictures.

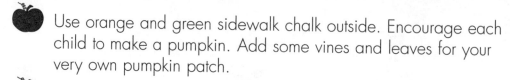 Use orange and green sidewalk chalk outside. Encourage each child to make a pumpkin. Add some vines and leaves for your very own pumpkin patch.

Make your own patterns for rubbings by cutting pumpkin shapes from textured items such as sandpaper or corrugated cardboard. Glue the textured shapes to a piece of cardboard. Show children how to place paper over the patterns and rub with the sides of chubby crayons (paper removed) until the patterns appear. A clipboard helps hold papers firmly.

Teach children the Pumpkinseed Game. Divide children into groups of three or four. Give each group about 20 pumpkin seeds and a cup or bowl and give each child a straw. Children will try to pick up the seeds by sucking through the straws and deposit the seeds into the cups. The first team to finish wins.

Another fun pumpkin game is Drop the Pumpkin Seeds. Provide a plastic jack-o'-lantern or other pumpkin-shaped bowl and invite each child to drop ten seeds from nose-height into the container. Count the number of seeds in the bowl when each child finishes.

ARTS AND CRAFTS

Provide orange paint at the easel and encourage children to make large orange circles (pumpkins). Have them fill in the circles completely. After the orange has dried, put out green and brown paint and have children add stems and leaves. Provide a real pumpkin for children to observe as they paint.

While the orange paint is out, children may enjoy painting numbers, names, letters of the alphabet, spelling words, or number words.

Make a bulletin board entitled "You Are the Pumpkin in My Patch!" Give each child a glob of red fingerpaint and a glob of yellow fingerpaint to mix together on fingerpaint paper. When they have covered the paper, have children cut out large pumpkin shapes from white construction paper to press over the still-wet fingerpaintings to make prints. Let the pumpkin prints dry and discard the fingerpaintings. Add green stems and leaves cut from construction paper and some green curling ribbon. Create a pumpkin patch by mounting the pumpkins against a dark blue or black background. Add student-cut stars to the top of the bulletin board.

Pre-cut a pumpkin shape for each child from yellow construction paper or use small paper plates. Provide torn strips of orange construction paper in several shades. Encourage children to tear the strips into small pieces and cover the yellow pumpkins by gluing on bits of orange paper. When children have covered their pumpkins, provide scraps of green and brown to make stems and leaves.

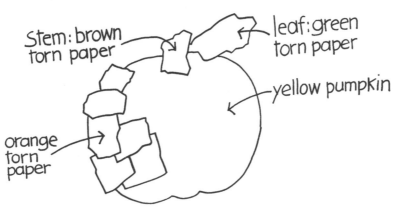

● Make a papier mâché pumpkin piñata to use at a Pumpkin Party. Blow up a large balloon. Soak hand-sized pieces of newspaper in wallpaper paste. Apply two to five layers of newspaper to the balloon until it is completely covered, smoothing wrinkles as you go. After it has dried for two or three days, paint it orange and hang from the ceiling with green curling ribbon. To use as a piñata, leave a small area at the top uncovered and work in a paper clip bent into an S. When the papier mâché has dried, pop the balloon, paint the pumpkin, and fill it with orange candies. Hang the piñata from the ceiling or outside from a tree limb. With children sitting at a safe distance, give one child a broomstick or heavy yard/meter stick, spin the child three or four times, and give him or her three attempts to break the piñata. You may wish to blindfold older children. Give different children turns until the piñata breaks. Be sure to have enough treats for each child. You may wish to label the treats with children's names.

● Give each child two heavy paper plates and have children paint the *bottoms* of the two plates orange. When they are dry, staple the plates together bottom-sides out, adding green or brown construction paper stems, green leaves, and a little green curling ribbon. Hang from the ceiling.

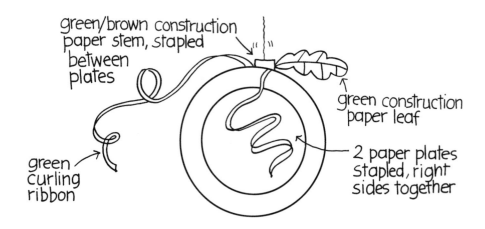

green/brown construction paper stem, stapled between plates

green construction paper leaf

green curling ribbon

2 paper plates stapled, right sides together

Make fall pumpkin wreaths using paper plates with the centers cut out as frames. Have children use pencils to draw pumpkins on orange construction paper (use several shades of orange if you can) and then cut them out. Use green construction paper for leaves and stems and add a little green curling ribbon for pieces of vine. Have children glue the pumpkins around the paper-plate frames. You may wish to add some full colored leaves cut from construction paper as well. Or use die-cut pumpkins and leaves. A paper clip taped to the underside makes a nice hanger. If you like, add a raffia bow.

 Make pumpkin hats using pumpkin cutouts (die-cut pumpkins, cut from stencils or patterns, or hand-drawn, colored, and cut out). Glue pumpkins to sentence strips. Staple the ends of the sentence strips together, measuring the circumference of each child's head to make pumpkin hats. Add a little green curling ribbon to stems.

 Make pumpkin centerpieces. Cut two pumpkin shapes from white construction paper for each child or have children cut their own. Show children how to sponge-paint both pumpkins (one side only) using pieces of sponge attached to clothespins and orange paint (or cut the pumpkins from orange construction paper). Sprinkle glitter on pumpkins while still wet. When dry, insert stems cut from brown or green construction paper between the pumpkin shapes as you glue them back-to-back. Add craft sticks, tongue depressors, or rolled paper sticks to the bottoms of the pumpkins.

Place a little green curling ribbon by the stems and green/orange/yellow curling ribbon bows under each pumpkin. Put several pumpkins in a flowerpot, which may be painted or sponged with pumpkin and leaf shapes. To help the pumpkins stay firmly in the pot, insert a Styrofoam® bowl upside down in the bottom of the flowerpot and push the pumpkin sticks through the Styrofoam. Fill the pot with Easter grass, straw, or Spanish moss. Makes a great centerpiece for Fall Open House or for a "Pumpkin Luncheon" for parents.

For a beautiful Thanksgiving centerpiece, turn a pumpkin into a turkey. Choose a well-shaped, medium-sized pumpkin. For the head, cut two head-and-neck shapes from felt and hot glue edges together with a little batting in between to give some dimension. Add features by hot gluing pieces of felt for eyes, beak, and wattle. Use round-headed pins to attach the head to the pumpkin. For the tail, insert eucalyptus, branches of autumn leaves, or wooden skewers with fall-colored paper leaves attached into the back of the "turkey." Place on a tray and add autumn leaves or assorted nuts in shells.

90

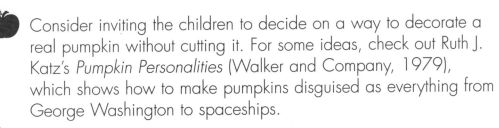 Consider inviting the children to decide on a way to decorate a real pumpkin without cutting it. For some ideas, check out Ruth J. Katz's *Pumpkin Personalities* (Walker and Company, 1979), which shows how to make pumpkins disguised as everything from George Washington to spaceships.

Look for the pumpkin sticker kits now available for decorating pumpkins without cutting them. The stickers can also be used on paper cutout pumpkins. Consider buying some kits on sale after the season to use next year.

Cut a face into your pumpkin to make a jack-o'-lantern. "Jack-o'-lantern" comes from an old Irish fable about a mean, stingy man named Jack who lived a wicked life. According to legend, he was condemned to walk the earth until Judgment Day, so he cut some holes in a pumpkin (some versions say he first used a turnip or potato) and put a hot coal inside to light his way in the darkness. He was called "Jack of the Lantern," which was soon shortened to jack-o'-lantern. Let your children design their own jack-o'-lanterns to light the way in the darkness. Look for any of the many pumpkin-carving kits now available or try some of the patterns from *You Can Carve a Fantastic Jack-o'-lantern* by Rhonda Massingham Hart (Garden Way Publishing, 1989). Have children vote on their favorite pumpkin design before cutting. After you have carved the jack-o'-lantern, encourage children to dictate sentences describing the sequence of events using the words *first, next, and then*, and *finally*. Children will also enjoy the simple board book *Jack-o'-lantern* by Kathie B. Smith (MJ Studios), which describes buying the pumpkin, cutting the face, and adding the candle.

FIELD STUDY

Visit a farmer's market, roadside stand, or grocery store to purchase a pumpkin for the class. Before buying the pumpkin, ask the children to bring in pennies to pay for it. Keep the pennies in a large plastic bowl, so children can watch them accumulate. On the specified day, have children guess how many pennies are in the bowl. Write their estimates down so you can compare the estimates with the actual number. Have children sort the pennies into stacks of ten and then roll ten stacks into penny wrappers. Check ahead to be sure the seller will accept rolled pennies.

Read *The Pumpkin Patch* by Patricia Miles Martin (G. P. Putnam's Sons, 1966), the story of a class field trip to a pumpkin patch, and *Picking Apples and Pumpkins* by Amy and Richard Hutchings (Scholastic, 1994), the story of a family that picks apples and gathers pumpkins on a fall afternoon. Beautiful photographs capture the colors of the season. A favorite for the youngest reader is Anne Rockwell's *Apples and Pumpkins* (with illustrations by her daughter, Lizzy), which tells in the simplest language of a family trip to Comstock Farm, where the leaves turn red and yellow and you know it is time to pick apples and pumpkins.

Visit a "pick-your-own" pumpkin farm. Arrange for a farmer to explain to children how pumpkins grow. Be sure to observe the different colors and shapes of pumpkins. Have the class choose a pumpkin to take back with them. If the farmer is willing, encourage children to feel the leaves and vines in the pumpkin patch.

Use a computer program to create a thank-you banner for your trip. Have children draw pumpkins on the printed banner and sign their names or add orange fingerprints by their pictures. Send the banner to the farmer.

When you get back to school, ask each child to complete the sentence, "At the pumpkin farm, I saw _____" on a sentence strip. Invite children to illustrate their sentences on index cards and glue the cards to the ends of the sentence strips. Bind the sentence strips together by punching holes at the ends, add a cover strip, and join with a ring binder to make a class field-experience book.

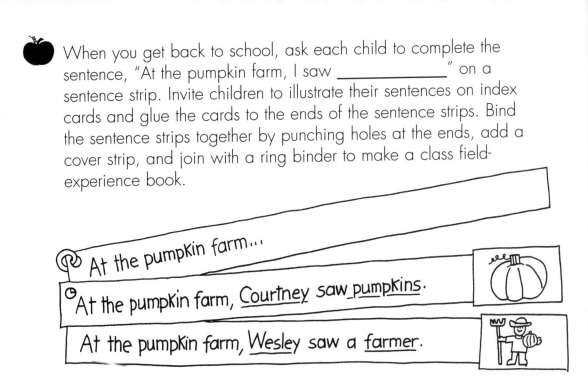

At the pumpkin farm...

At the pumpkin farm, <u>Courtney</u> saw <u>pumpkins</u>.

At the pumpkin farm, <u>Wesley</u> saw a <u>farmer</u>.

These days, many families own video cameras. Ask a parent volunteer to tape the field trip, so you may enjoy the experience with your class over and over. Children love seeing themselves on TV. If you have a video camera available in the classroom, add some footage of the children carving and enjoying the pumpkin they purchased and other pumpkin-related activities you may do. Send the video home with individual children to enjoy with their families.

PARENT CONNECTION

Invite parents to come in at the end of your unit to share some of the things you have been studying. They might stay for a few extra minutes in the morning, come for brunch or after lunch, arrive a little early for dismissal, or come in the evening. Consider some of the following ideas for a Pumpkin Party.

INVITATIONS

- Have children make pumpkin-shaped invitations to invite families to a Pumpkin Party.
- Consider including some members of the school staff in your guest list.

DECORATING THE ROOM

- Take photographs as you are working through the unit to place around the room. Nothing is a better ice breaker than photographs of children.
- Decorate the room with pumpkin projects the class has completed, such as art projects, big books, and individual books. Use the centerpiece and wreath ideas in the Arts and Crafts section (see page 89).

DECORATING THE CHILDREN

- Consider having children make pumpkin or fall T-shirts. Ask each child to bring in a plain white T-shirt. Help them use acrylic paint and pumpkin and leaf-shaped sponges to sponge-print pumpkins and autumn leaves in orange, red, yellow, and brown on their T-shirts.
- Invite each child to make a pumpkin hat to wear on the special day (see page 89).

94

REFRESHMENTS

• Have children prepare a pumpkin snack ahead of time. Yummy Pumpkin Muffins or Pumpkin Pie are good choices. Serve with a little apple juice and popcorn for a seasonal treat.

• If you sponge-print T-shirts with children, you may choose to print some leaves or pumpkins on cups, napkins, paper plates, or a white paper tablecloth as well.

 ENTERTAINMENT

• Have children perform a few pumpkin songs or fingerplays they have learned in this unit.

• Invite children to act out a book or song that you have studied.

• Make large letter cards for *P-U-M-P-K-I-N* and encourage children to hold the letters and recite one of the best acrostic poems (*P* is for perfect pumpkin pie, *U* is for . . .).

• Consider videotaping children performing the previous suggestions and showing the video at the party instead of having children perform live. Or simply tape the children working individually or in groups to share some of the activities you have been doing.

For teachers who are uncomfortable with parents in their classroom:

• Videotape the different activities you do in class. At the end of the unit, send the Pumpkin Video home for a night (check-out) with each member of the class. What a wonderful language activity—children share all they have learned about pumpkins as they watch the video with their families.

• Make *several* class big books while working on this unit. As each is complete, encourage individual children to check them out for the night to share with families.

The main idea is to share with parents something about what their children are learning. It doesn't really matter *how* you share or exactly *what* you share—as long as you offer families an opportunity to get involved with their children's educations.

INDEX

To order small apple and pumpkin erasers and other small seasonal things to use as counters and markers, try

Oriental Trading Company, Inc.
P.O. Box 3407
Omaha, NE 68103–0407

For die-cut apple and pumpkin-shaped notepads, try your local school-supply store or

Shapes Etc.
8840 Route 36
P.O. Box 400
Dansville, NY 14437
1–800–888–6580
FAX 716–335–6070

Carson-Dellosa Publishing Company
P.O. Box 35665
Greensboro, NC 27425
1–800–321–0943

For apple and pumpkin charts and chartlets, traditional and pop-out borders, bulletin board pieces, memo boards, clock decorations, self-stick notelets, calendar pieces, and stickers, check with your local school-supply store or try

Carson-Dellosa Publishing Company
P.O. Box 35665
Greensboro, NC 27425
1–800–321–0943